Raffael und seine Zeit / Raphael And His Time

Herausgegeben von / Edited by Jürg Meyer zur Capellen

Band/Vol. 1

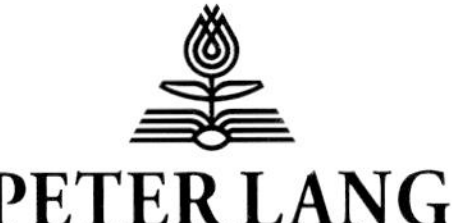

PETER LANG

Frankfurt am Main · Berlin · Bern · Bruxelles · New York · Oxford · Wien

Jürg Meyer zur Capellen
Claudio Falcucci

The *Portrait of Baldassare Castiglione* & the *Madonna dell'Impannata Northwick*
Two Studies on Raphael

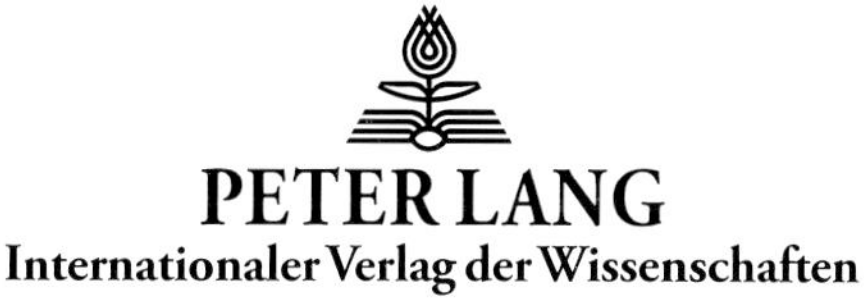

PETER LANG
Internationaler Verlag der Wissenschaften

Bibliographic Information published by the Deutsche Nationalbibliothek
The Deutsche Nationalbibliothek lists this publication in the Deutsche
Nationalbibliografie; detailed bibliographic data is available in the internet
at http://dnb.d-nb.de.

Cover Illustration:
Raphael, Portrait of Baldassare Castiglione. Paris, Louvre, inv. 611
Workshop of Raphael, Madonnna dell'Impannata. Private Collection

Translations from German to English:
Michael Foster (Baldassare Castiglione and Studies
on the Madonna dell'Impannata II.)
Stefan Polter (Studies on the Madonna dell'Impannata I. and III.)

Editing and Layout:
Katrin Heusing

ISSN 2192-9742
ISBN 978-3-631- 62140-0

© Peter Lang GmbH
Internationaler Verlag der Wissenschaften
Frankfurt am Main 2011
Alle Rechte vorbehalten.

www.peterlang.de

Contents

PREFACE

The series RAPHAEL AND HIS TIME is devoted to single works or œuvres in the visual arts realized by Raphael and by his contemporaries and immediate successors. The papers are aiming at the monographic investigation of painting, drawing, and printing basing on the variety of the methodological analysis. Particular stress will be laid on technological investigation.

VORWORT

Die Schriftenreihe RAFFAEL UND SEINE ZEIT dient der Veröffentlichung von Untersuchungen zu Einzel- und Gesamtwerken von Raffael, von seinen Zeitgenossen und seinen unmittelbaren Nachfolgern. Die Beiträge betreffen sowohl Werke der Malerei als auch der Zeichnung und der Druckgraphik. Sie sind einer Methodenvielfalt verpflichtet, wobei ein besonderer Akzent auf technologische Analysen gelegt wird.

August 2011 *Jürg Meyer zur Capellen*

BALDASSARE CASTIGLIONE and ANTONIO TEBALDEO
Raphael Portrays Two of His Friends

In his Roman period Raphael maintained close relations with Baldassare Castiglione, one of the outstanding humanists associated with the court of Pope Leo X. The artist's well-known portrait of Castiglione, now in the Louvre in Paris, testifies to their friendship and its intended audience presumably consisted of members of the papal court circle, who included sophisticated lovers of art learned enough to appreciate such a complex work. Given this context, the portrait probably represented a combined effort on the part of the artist and his sitter.

Baldassare Castiglione (1478–1529) came from a minor aristocratic family based near Mantua.[1] Most of its male members devoted themselves to warfare, and Castiglione obviously received a thorough training in this field. In the course of his life he took part in various military campaigns, distinguishing himself on several occasions. The head of some campaigns, Francesco Maria della Rovere, duke of Urbino, rewarded him with the hereditary principality of Novilara for his services. Castiglione was also entrusted with important diplomatic missions. In 1506 Guidobaldo da Montefeltro sent him to England to receive the Order of the Garter from Henry VII on his behalf. From 1514 he resided in Rome as the *oratore* (spokesman) of the duke of Urbino. In 1516 he married Ippolita Torelli of the Bentivoglio family, with whom he had two children. On the death of Lorenzo de' Medici, who had occupied Urbino at the behest of Pope Leo X,

---

1   For Castiglione, see C. MUTINI in: *Dizionario biografico degli Italiani*, vol. 22, Rome 1979, pp. 53–68, and WALTER BARBERIS, ed., *Baldassare Castiglione: Il libro del cortegiano*, Turin 1998, both with extensive bibliographies. Many aspects of Castiglione's career are addressed by ROBERT W. HANNING and DAVID ROSAND, *Castiglione: The Ideal and the Real in Renaissance Culture*, New Haven and London 1983.

the ousted Francesco Maria della Rovere commissioned Castiglione to promote his reinstatement as duke of Urbino at the papal court, a task he continued after Leo X's death and Cardinal Giulio de' Medici's election on 15 November 1523 as Pope Clement VII. The climax of Castiglione's career came in 1525, when he was despatched on a mission to the imperial court in Toledo. When he died there unexpectedly on 7 February 1529, aged fifty, Emperor Charles V informed his court: *'Yo vos digo que es muerto uno de los mejores caballeros del mundo'* (*I tell you that one of the finest gentlemen in the world has died*).[2] The Spanish term *caballero* (gentleman, knight) seems basically to have corresponded to the Italian *cortegiano* (gentleman, courtier), but possessed stronger military connotations.

If contemporaries saw Castiglione principally as a soldier and a diplomat, today he is known above all as the learned and influential humanist who wrote *Il libro del cortegiano* (*The Book of the Courtier*). On settling in Rome he made friends with many leading figures, including Pietro Bembo, Jacopo Sadoleto and Bernardo Dovizi da Bibbiena among the humanists and Raphael and Michelangelo among the artists. At this time he was already working on *Il libro del cortegiano*, in which he defined the ideal courtier by means of fictitious conversations between members of the current court at Urbino.[3] By 1518 he had finished the second, revised version of the *Cortegiano* and sent copies to some friends, including Bembo. In 1527 he dispatched the final manuscript to the printer in Venice and began distributing copies the following year. Since he died in 1529, the full effect of the work was not felt until after its author's death.

In his portrait of *c.* 1514-15 Raphael shows his friend as a half-length figure casting a shadow on the right of the grey wall behind him (fig. 1). Castiglione, presumably sitting in a Savonarola chair, gazes calmly at the viewer. His winter

---

2   Quoted in BARBERIS, op. cit. (note 1), p. XC.
3   For the figures involved, see BARBERIS, op. cit. (note 1), pp. 24f.

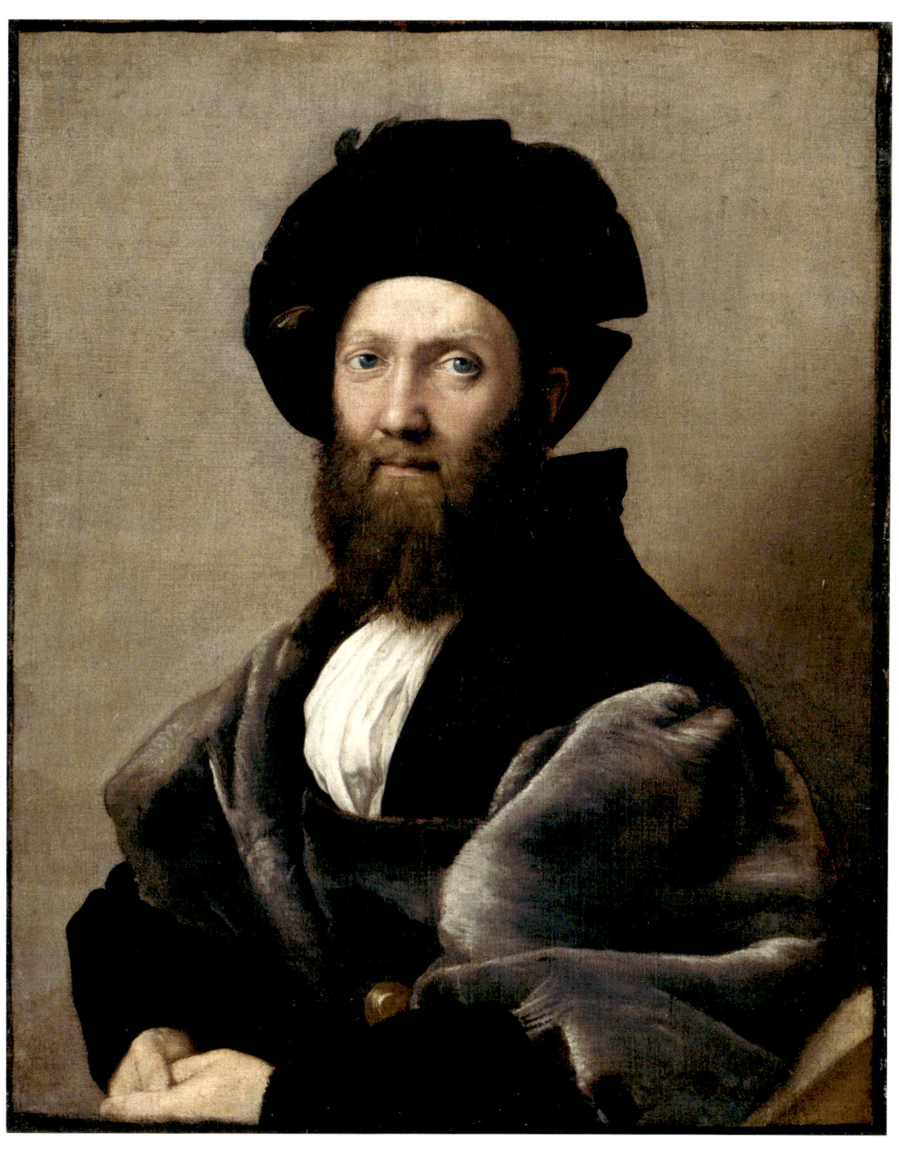

1   Raphael, *Portrait of Baldassare Castiglione*, ca. 1514-15, canvas, 82 x 67 cm, Paris, Musée du Louvre.

clothing is as elegant as it is striking: over a pleated shirt he wears a dark doublet combined with grey cropped fur,[4] from which the pommel of a dagger emerges at the chest. His hands, cut off at the lower edge of the painting, are folded. The sitter's well-proportioned features are framed by a full, well-kept beard; his cheeks are slightly red. His eyes shine beneath light-toned eyebrows, the pupils shifted to one side. A bold but not insistent note is struck by the strong, straight nose and by the closed mouth, over which the trace of a smile seems to flicker. The top of the head is covered by a close-fitting netted cap called a *scuffiotto*, over which Castioglione wears a large, dark *biretta* decorated with a badge that shines forth from the shade. It may be assumed that the sitter chose the apparel in which he wished to be depicted, since it both corresponds to his notion of the attire appropriate to a *cortegiano* and reflects to a certain extent his penchant for extravagance.[5] The choice of winter clothing doubtless resulted from his preference for dark colours[6] and underscores the muted character of the image as a whole.

The portrait represents not only a notably self-possessed image of Castiglione, but also the qualities allegedly required by the ideal courtier. The flash of the dagger pommel alludes, almost incidentally, to the virtue of *fortitudo* (fortitude) and thus to Castiglione's military prowess, an accomplishment particularly valued by his contemporaries.[7] On the other hand, the confident pose, calm and collected, and the firm gaze emphasise both *prudentia* (prudence) and *temperantia*

4　Commentators have offered very different descriptions of the clothing. Sylvie béguin (*Raphael dans les collections françaises*, Paris 1983, p. 87), for example, identified the grey sections as cropped beaver fur, while Oskar Fischel (*Raphael*, vol. 1, Paris 1948, p. 117) saw them as velvet.

5　Castiglione includes a discussion of the dress suitable to the (ideal) courtier in Book 2 of *Il cortegiano*, especially in chapters 26 and 27. See Barberis, op. cit. (note 1), pp. 156f.

6　See mutini, op. cit. (note 1), p. 54, who quotes briefly from surviving documents to describe the clothing favoured by Castiglione.

7　john r. hale in hanning and rosand, op. cit. (note 1), pp. 143–164.

(temperance). In presenting this image of himself Castiglione will have taken to heart Cicero's words in *De oratore* (*On Oratory*) admonishing speakers not to mime their thoughts, but merely to suggest them in bearing and gesture. At one point Cicero writes: *'But all depends upon the face, and the power of the face is centred in the eyes.… It is by the steadfastness, by the abashment of the eye, by a downcast or a cheerful look, that we … accommodate what we say to what we feel.'*[8] Taking their cue from portraiture in classical antiquity, which apparently echoed Cicero's advice,[9] it is easy to imagine the humanist Castiglione and the artist Raphael joining forces to work out the ideas encapsulated in the portrait. Seen in these terms, the careful balance of elegance and dignity, of alertness and sovereign calm, must appear as typical of the intellectual and physical qualities both of this particular individual and of his social class as a whole.

In a sense the image culminates in the striking *biretta*. Among other things, this headgear served to mask Castiglione's incipient baldness. A balding sitter could scarcely personify the notion of the perfect courtier as someone who possessed a dignified and flawless appearance.[10] The details, and hence the full significance, of the badge flashing against the dark background of the *biretta* cannot be made out. Philipp Fehl is doubtless correct to see in it an embodiment of *sprezzatura* (nonchalance),[11] which Castiglione thought the *cortegiano* should cultivate in contrast to *affettazione* (affectation).[12] *Sprezzatura* revealed itself principally in small matters and had an equivalent in painting in *licenzia* (licence, freedom). *Sprezzatura* might entail mentioning important aspects of

---

8   MARCUS TULLIUS CICERO, *De oratore*, trans. William Guthrie as *M.T. Cicero, or his Three Dialogues upon the Character and Qualifications of an Orator*, Boston 1822, pp. 342f.

9   See LUCA GIULIANI, *Bildnis und Botschaft*, Frankfurt am Main 1986, esp. pp. 97–100.

10 See note 4.

11 PHILIPP FEHL, *Sprezzatura and the Art of Painting Finely*, Groningen 1997, p. 11.

12 See EDUARDO SACCONE, *'Grazia, Sprezzatura, Affettazione in the Courtier'*, in HANNING and ROSAND, op. cit. (note 1) esp. p. 62.

one's activities only in passing. Transferred to the medium of painting, this could have meant limiting symbolic references to cursory allusions. In the portrait this would explain why the dagger is only hinted at by the pommel and why the badge is barely distinguishable from the *biretta*. Since Castiglione and his friends and acquaintances, including Raphael, would have known the badge and the personal device it doubtless bore, the painting need do no more than suggest its presence. Castiglione clearly had no intention of using the portrait to acquaint others with his personal device.

An elegy by Castiglione contains a letter purportedly written to him by his wife. This stresses the lifelike quality of the portrait, with which Ippolita and the couple's young son commune as consolation during his frequent absences.[13] Today it is generally assumed that the 'letter' is the work of Castiglione himself, and the touching domestic scenes it depicts are thus presumably a literary invention rather than a description of reality.[14] Castiglione's emphasis on likeness (*similtudo*) – which had been cited by Alberti as an essential ingredient of portraiture[15] – may also be interpreted as the

---

13 JOHN SHEARMAN, *Raphael in Early Modern Sources*, New Haven and London 2003, vol. 1, pp. 495–500. See also ibid., pp. 498–500, for a translation of the passage and the identification of the portrait. The present author believes Shearman is correct to equate it with the painting now in the Louvre.

14 Many notably vivid descriptions in Castiglione's works are also probably fictitious. Renaissance authors customarily employed such inventions as a means of enlivening their writings. See PAUL BAROLSKY, *Why Mona Lisa Smiles and Other Tales by Vasari*, University Park, Pennsylvania, 1991, in which the author cites some amusing examples to indicate that Vasari saw himself principally as a literary figure when writing his *Vite de' più eccellenti pittori, scultori et architettori* (see note 39).

15 See LEON BATTISTA ALBERTI, *De Statua, De Pictura, Elementa Picturae*, ed. OSKAR BÄTSCHMANN and CHRISTOPH SCHÄUBLIN, Darmstadt 2000 (Latin and German). The relevant remarks appear in chapters 4 and 5 of the book on statues; ibid., pp. 147–153. For a discussion of Alberti's use of the term *similtudo*, see EDOUARD POMMIER, *Storia e teoria del Rinascimento all'Età dei Lumi*, trans. from the French by Michela Scolaro, Turin 1998, pp. 30–33. LUIGI GRASSI and MARIO PEPE discuss *similtudo* under 'Somiglianza'

kind of understatement allegedly typical of the ideal courtier, for the portrait is too finely wrought to have been viewed solely in these terms. In fact, it can be assumed that the learned humanist Castiglione saw the aspects of the painting outlined above in the context of his *Libro del cortegiano*, which he was revising for the first time when the portrait was painted *c.* 1514–15. Anyone familiar with *Il cortegiano* will easily recognise references in the portrait to the sitter's *virtutes* (virtues). However, by the time the book became so widely read as virtually to constitute a courtier's manual, Castiglione was dead and the portrait no longer accessible. Indeed, the painting's whereabouts before 1639, when it is recorded in the collection of Lucas van Uffelen in Amsterdam, cannot be ascertained.[16]

A portrait of Castiglione now in the Galleria Nazionale, Rome, although still occasionally described as a copy of the Louvre painting, evinces a rather different character (fig. 2).[17] With respect to viewpoint, clothing and facial features it resembles Raphael's painting, but the lack of *scuffiotto* and *biretta* alters the impact of the physiognomy by exposing Castiglione's

---

in: *Dizionario della critica d'arte*, Turin 1978, pp. 551f. It should not be forgotten that the term *similtudo* tended to be used as a *topos* in Renaissance writing on art rather than as a word signifying 'likeness' in the modern sense. This aspect was addressed by LINDA KLINGER in the paper 'The "Fact" of Likeness in Renaissance Portraiture', given at the symposium *Portraits of the Ottoman Sultans: The Penultimate Cut*, held in Oxford from 27 to 29 March 1995. It has not been possible to ascertain whether the paper has been published in the form of an article.

16 No known engravings or copies, for example, can be dated with certainty to earlier than the mid-seventeenth century.

17 SHEARMAN, op. cit. (note 13), p. 241. Information on the portrait is provided by BEFFA NEGRINI, *Elogi historici*, 1606 (see Shearman, vol. 2, pp. 1402-1405); GUIDO LA ROCCA, 'I ritratti di Baldassare Castiglione', in: UBALDO MERONI, *Il ritratto antico illustrato*, N. 1, Monzambano 1984, pp. 61–72; and NOVELLA MACOLA in: PINA RAGIONIERI, *Vittoria Colonna e Michelangelo*, Florence 2005, pp. 58–60. The Louvre possesses another version of the Roman portrait (acc. RF 204), though without the inscription, which is discussed below. BÉGUIN, op. cit. (note 4), no. 27, pp. 126f., rightly insisted that this Louvre painting cannot be a copy of Raphael's portrait.

incipient baldness. With good reason, the portrait has recently been attributed to Giulio Romano.[18] In the present author's opinion the similarities between the two images can best be explained by the existence of a common model by Raphael, which the Rome painting reproduces faithfully in all essentials.

Comparison of the Louvre version with that in Rome reveals how strongly the former sacrifices realism to idealisation. Naturalistic elements, such as the receding hair and the rather sharp gaze, figure prominently in the Rome portrait. In addition, the eyes and the mouth, surrounded by the beard, lack the gentle calm of the painting in the Louvre. Significantly, the pleated shirt and the black doublet are largely similar in both versions. This suggests that Castiglione sat for his friend dressed in the simple clothes depicted in the Rome portrait. The fur would then have been added in the Louvre painting and the figure shown at a greater distance from the viewer. Both aspects doubtless resulted from the patron's desire for a more prestigious image. In this connection it is worth noting that the fur would never have been worn in the way indicated in the painting. It could not have been draped over Castiglione's right shoulder if, as depicted, it were attached directly to the doublet at the left shoulder. Raphael obviously arranged it purely in terms of his composition. Moreover, it seems that he added the section around the left shoulder at a relatively late stage: this area has become worn over time and the black of the doublet underneath now shows through the fur.[19]

---

18 TULLIA CARRATÙ in: SYLVESTRE VERGER and PATRIZIA NITTI, *Titien: Le pouvoir en face*, Paris 2006, pp. 174f. (with bibliography).

19 Red chalk underdrawing – which infra-red reflectography naturally cannot disclose – has apparently been discovered in this area. This information has been provided by Vincent Delieuvin in connection with the Raphael exhibition being organised by the Louvre in association with the Prado, Madrid, and scheduled to take place in 2012. In particular, the exhibition will reveal the results of scientific examinations conducted over an extended period on Raphael's paintings of 1510–20.

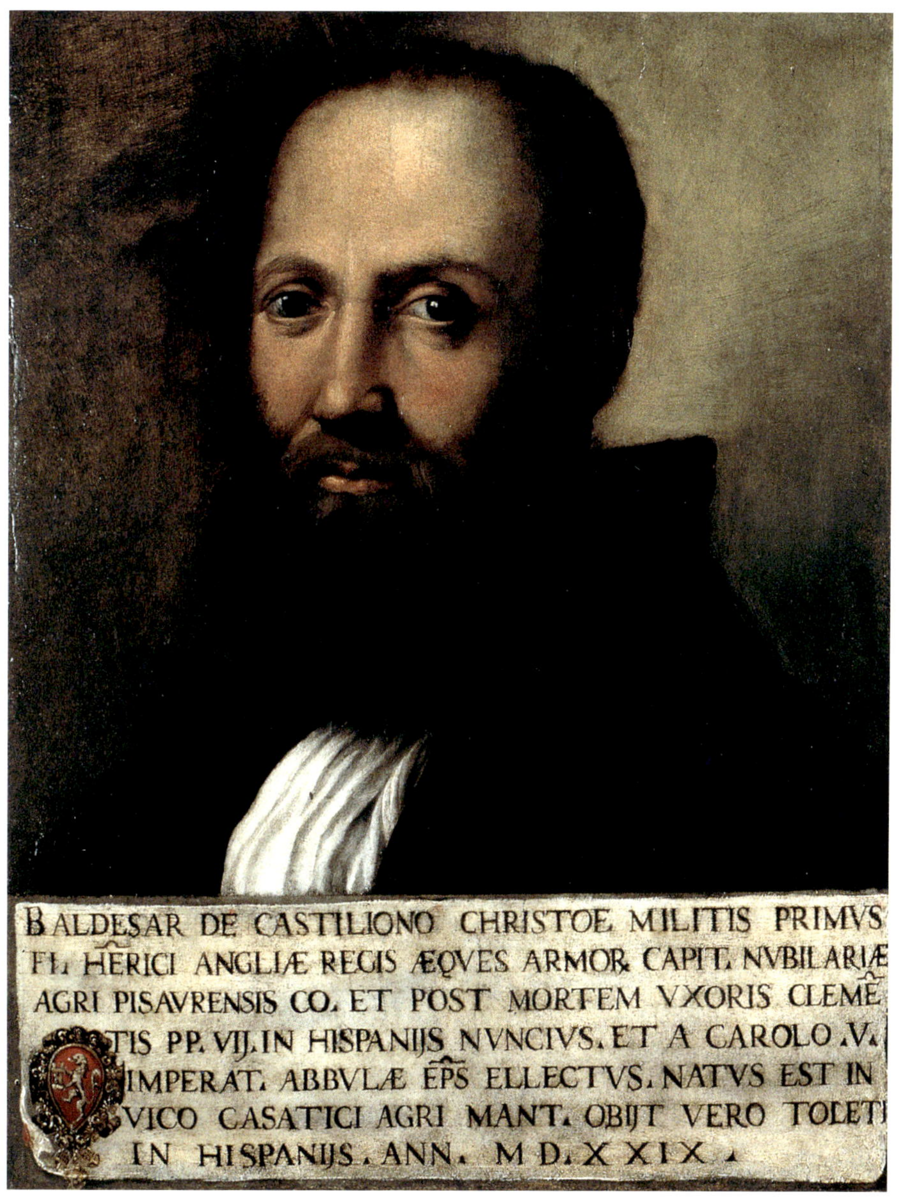

2   Giulio Romano (?) after Raphael, *Portrait of Baldassare Castiglione*, ca. 1530, canvas, 54 x 42 cm, Rome, Galleria Nazionale d'Arte Antica.

There are good reasons to suppose that the portrait in Rome was owned by the Castiglione family. Why were they satisfied with a naturalistic image that did not embody the sitter's characteristic *virtutes*? For them, the portrait probably functioned as a memorial: it offered a precise record of Castiglione's appearance and alluded to the virtues apparent from his career in the inscription at the bottom, which includes his date of death along with the family coat of arms: 'BALDESAR DE CASTILIONO CHRISTOF. MILITIS PRIMVS / FI. HE[N]RICI ANGLIAE REGIS AEQUES ARMOR[UM] CAPT. NVBILIARE / AGRI PISAVRENSIS CO. ET POST MORTEM VXORIS CLEME[N]TIS PP. VIJ. IN HISPANIJS NVNCIVS. ET A CAROLO. V. / IMPERAT. ABBVLAE EP[ISCOPU]S ELLECTVUS. NATVS EST IN / VICO CASATICI AGRI MANT. OBIJT VERO TOLETI / IN HISPANIJS ANN. MD.XXIX.'[20] The very first line of the inscription refers to the sitter's military accomplishments. This comes as no surprise in a family traditionally associated with warfare. Castiglione's son Camillo, for example, commissioned a medal of himself that showed him in profile wearing armour.[21] The inscription also cites Castiglione's missions to Henry VII of England and Charles V of Spain, which the family clearly saw as their famous member's most outstanding achievements. On the other hand, no mention is made of his activity as a writer and prominent humanist.

Juxtaposition of these two images of Castiglione shows that, while probably derived from the same model, they inhabit very different historical contexts, an aspect that will be discussed below in connection with Raphael's portrait of Tebaldeo. A third portrait of Castiglione, different again, appears on a medal, with a depiction of Aurora (Dawn) on the

---

20 See also CARRATÙ, op. cit. (note 18).

21 See GEORGE FRANCIS HILL and GRAHAM POLLARD, *Renaissance Medals from the Samuel H. Kress Collection in the National Gallery of Art*, London 1967, no. 321, p. 61. For Camillo Castiglione (1520–1598), who led a turbulent life in which military campaigns played a significant part, see G. DE CARO in: *Dizionario biografico degli Italiani*, vol. 22, Rome 1979, pp. 75f.

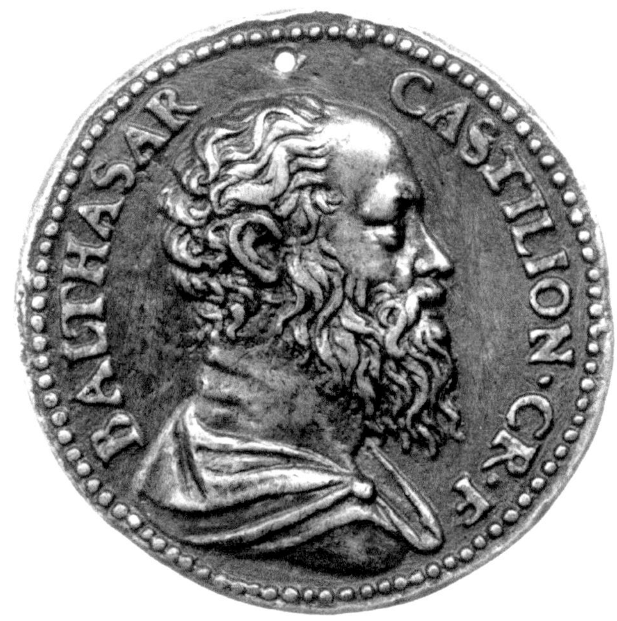

3   Anonymous,
    Portrait of
    Baldassare Castiglione,
    obverse of medal,
    diameter 3,7 cm.

reverse (fig. 3).[22] Although repeatedly associated with Raphael, the medal has been attributed to Giulio Romano by Shearman, who dates it to the early 1520s, pointing out that Giulio seems to have enjoyed closer relations with Castiglione after Raphael's death, in 1520.[23] The portrait differs markedly from the others, evoking antique models and embracing *similtudo* to a greater extent in that it emphasises Castiglione's increasing baldness rather than covering it up or playing it down – a feature that does nothing to diminish the effectiveness of the image. In type, the portrait alludes directly to

22 GEORGES FRANCIS HILL, *A Corpus of Italian Medals of the Renaissance before Cellini*, London 1930, 2nd ed., London 1967, no. 1158, and HILL and POLLARD, op. cit. (note 21), no. 305. The medal was mentioned in the early seventeenth century by BEFFA NEGRINI, op. cit. (note 17); see SHEARMAN, op. cit. (note 13), vol. 2, p. 1403. There seems to exist another medal portrait, which was published by JULIA CARTWRIGHT, *Baldassare Castiglione. The Perfect Courtier and His Life and Letters*, New York 1908, vol. 2, p. 448. The print after this medal, which might not exist any more, shows Castiglione in profile but considerably younger.

23 JOHN SHEARMAN, 'Giulio Romano and Castiglione', in: ORIANNA BARACCHI et al., *Giulio Romano*, Mantua 1989, pp. 293–301.

those on Roman coins. Many such coins were in circulation at the time and were sought after as collector's items by humanists.[24] Furthermore, in 1517 Andrea Fulvio published his *Illustrium Imagines,* which made available a representative selection of coin portraits of Roman emperors in the shape of woodcut reproductions (fig. 4).[25] The kind of summary *all'antica* drapery depicted on the Castiglione medal figures on Roman coins

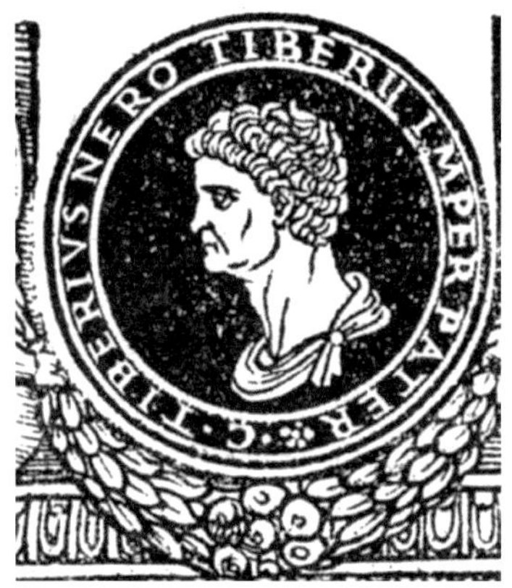

4 Andrea Fulvio, *Portrait of Claudius Tiberius Nero,* detail from *Illustrium Imagines* 1517.

and appears in similar, abbreviated form in the woodcuts in Fulvio's publication.[26] Although the medal portrait may be said to retain elements of *similtudo* despite the necessarily simplified features, far greater significance attaches to the fact that it is based on the familiar antique image of Socrates. This evocation of the famous philosopher embodies the medal's underlying message: as a humanist writer, Castiglione places himself in a line with the great ancient Greek thinker, his seemingly naturalistic image subtly ennobled by the classical reference.

---

24 Although the inventories of Castiglione's belongings drawn up after his death contain no references to antique coins, it may assumed that a learned humanist of his ilk possessed extensive knowledge of the portraits on such coins. For the inventories, see GUIDO REBECCHINI, 'The Book Collection and other Possessions of Baldassare Castiglione', in: *Journal of the Warburg and Courtauld Institutes,* vol. 61, 1998, pp. 17–52.

25 ANDREA FULVIO, *Illustrium Imagines,* Rome 1517, fol. XXVIII, repr. as vol. 9 in the series *The Printed Sources of Western Art,* ed. THEODORE BESTERMANN, Portland, Oregon, 1972. The detail reproduced here shows the portrait of Claudius Tiberius Nero, father of Emperor Tiberius.

26 Antique coin portraits show a far greater range of drapery depiction than the Fulvio woodcuts. The folds on the Castiglione medal closely resemble those in antique images of Antoninus Pius and the young Commodus. See RALPH KANKELFITZ, *Römische Münzen,* Augsburg 1996, pp. 148, 182.

The reverse of the medal is of special interest. It shows Aurora above a section of the globe and beneath the motto 'TEN-EBRARVM ET LVCIS' (fig. 5).[27] Hill and Pollard's explanation that the goddess symbolises Castiglione's 'culture' oversimplifies matters.[28] Fehl interpreted the phrase to mean that Aurora partakes of both light and dark, which might constitute a reference to the ups and downs of Castiglione's career.[29] In addition, Fehl saw Aurora as rising above northern Italy, a theory based on an engraving of the medal, which is more explicit than the original and does indeed depict Italy.[30] For Fehl, Aurora was also the *amica poetarum* (friend of poets) and he pointed by way of comparison to Raphael's *Poesia* in the Stanza della Segnatura in the Vatican, where the goddess appears on a pink cloud. Although this particular notion of Aurora is not documented *expressis verbis* until later, in Cesare Ripa's *Iconologia* of 1593,[31] the goddess was doubtless chosen for depiction on the medal by Castiglione as a way of evoking his activity as a poet. His special attachment to Aurora finds expression in the final section of *Il libro del corte-giano*, in which the distinguished guests, in the presence of the duchess, decide to continue their nocturnal deliberations on the following day, only to discover that night has already given way to dawn.

---

27 FEHL, op. cit. (note 11), p. 12, refers only to an engraving of the medal, which shows a section of the Mediterranean including Italy. HILL and POLLARD, op. cit. (note 21), recognise part of the Mediterranean in the section of earth shown on the medal. To the present author it seems that clouds are depicted at the top, with a form left of centre that might conceivably represent Italy.

28 HILL and POLLARD, op. cit. (note 21), and NEGRINI, op. cit. (note 17), pp. 430–432.

29 See SHEARMAN, op. cit. (note 23), pp. 294–296.

30 This is problematic, since the area of the globe shown on the medal is far less easily 'legible' than that in the engraving.

31 FEHL, op. cit. (note 11), p. 11. See SHEARMAN, op. cit. (note 23), no. 48, p. 301; GUY DE TERVARENT, 'Le Char de l'Aurore', in: *Attributs et symboles dans l'art profane*, Geneva 1958, repr. 1997, pp. 103f.; and idem, 'Les Rêves de l'Aurore', in: *Les Énigmes de l'Art: L'Héritage antique*, Paris 1946, pp. 58–64.

Shearman insists that Raphael played no part in the medal and points to its 'figural chiasmus' as a hallmark of Giulio Romano's style. Aurora, apparently alighting from her chariot, is flanked by two winged female figures who are bringing the horses under control. The poses and gestures of the figures generate a movement from left to right. An engraving of Aurora

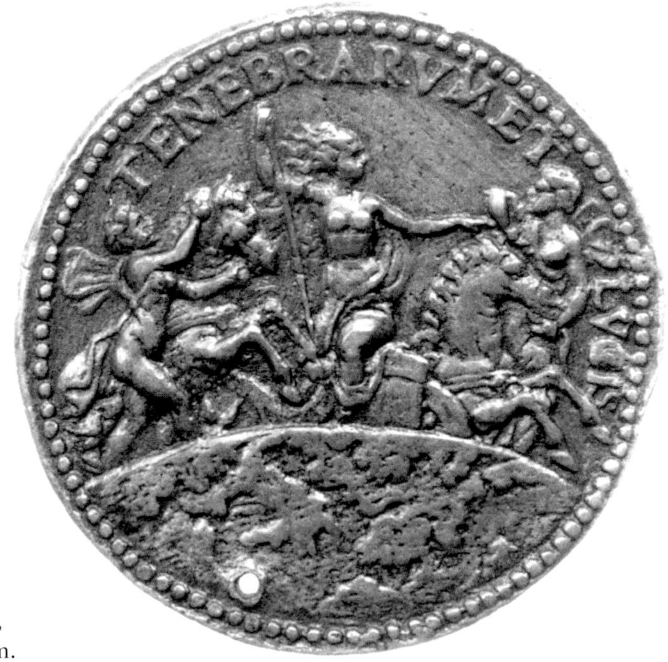

5　Anonymous,
Aurora,
revers of medal,
diameter 3,7 cm.

by Marcantonio Raimondi looks quite different (fig. 6). This shows the goddess just above the sea and in front of the rising sun. The clarity and harmony of the composition, despite its awkward rendering in the engraving, suggest that Raphael provided the model.[32] In terms of content, the image is obviously related closely to that on the medal. In Greek mythology

---

32　Raphael may well have based the composition on antique models, such as that on the Actium Cameo (Kunsthistorisches Museum, Vienna) or that on a cameo in Paris (Cabinet des Médailles, no. 267), which shows a frontal view of the goddess in her quadriga. My thanks to Wolf Rüdiger Megow for alerting me to these examples. These or comparable works known to Raphael doubtless provided him with nothing more than an initial stimulus.

Eos (the Roman Aurora) rises each morning from the bed of her husband, Tithonus, and, emerging with her horse-drawn chariot from the sea (Oceanus), leads the sun-god Helios across the heavens.[33] The two female figures accompanying Aurora on the medal have been identified as Psyches or Muses, yet general agreement on this does not exist.

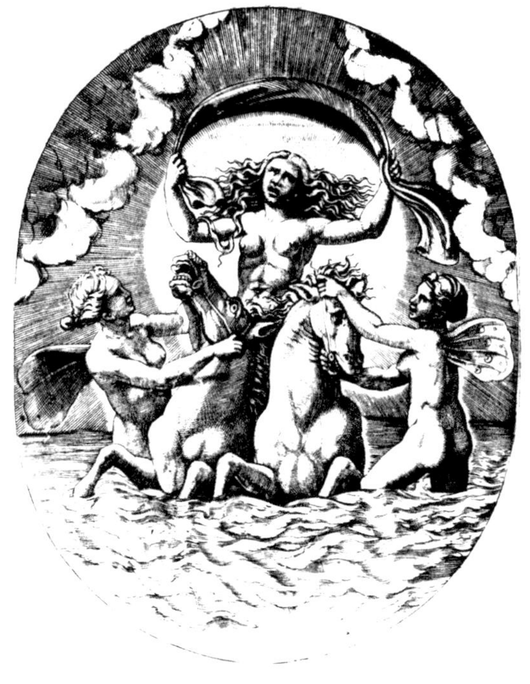

6   Marcantonio
Raimondi,
Aurora,
etching, 17 x 13,3 cm.

It should be noted that Aurora's companions sport the same wings as the Horae (Hours) shown scattering flowers in Raphael's *Feast of the Gods* in the Villa Farnesina, Rome, though the latter are clothed.[34] Close examination of the engraving reveals that these female figures are bridling the horses (fig. 7). This, too, identifies them as the Horae. Goddesses of nature, the Horae served or assisted other deities as their subordinates. In his *Metamorphoses* Ovid describes, for instance, how they attended

---

33 For Aurora, see 'Eos' in: W. H. ROSCHER, *Ausführliches Lexikon der griechischen und römischen Mythologie*, Leipzig 1884–86, vol. I.1, col. 1252–1278.

34 For an illustration, see ROSALIA VAROLI-PIAZZI, ed., *Raffaello: La loggia di Amore e Psiche alla Farnesina*, Milan 2002, p. 289.

to the horses of Helios: *'And when his father [Titan] saw the earth and the wide universe in glowing tints arrayed…he bade the nimble Hours to yoke the steeds.'*[35] They accompanied Aurora in their function as personifications of the times of day.[36] Quintus Smyrnaeus mentions them in this capacity in his Trojan epic *Posthomerica*: *'by command of Eos…Dawn divine now heavenward soared with the all-fostering Hours.'*[37] These two aspects serve to identify the figures and their activity both in the engraving and on the medal, where they are again bridling the horses (fig. 8). The engraving shows the winged Horae assisting Aurora as she rises from Oceanus in the morning, but on the medal, where they appear at either end of the earth, they perhaps personify both dawn and dusk. This would lend an iconographical dimension to Shearman's use of the term 'chiasmus' in connection with the style of the medal image.

In view of the close association between Castiglione and Aurora suggested by the goddess's appearance on the portrait medal it seems not unreasonable to conjecture that the badge featured in the Louvre painting also bore an image of this mythological figure. There, too, the motif may have taken the form probably invented by Raphael and documented in the engraving.

---

35 PUBLIUS OVIDIUS NASO, *Metamorphoses*, trans. Brookes More, Boston 1922, vol. 2, S. 115-121.

36 For the 'nature aspect' of the Horae, see ROSCHER, op. cit. (note 33), vol. I.2, col. 2721, which contains the reference to Quintus Smyrnaeus (see note 37). Roscher notes how notions of the Horae overlapped with those relating to the Hesperides.

37 QUINTUS SMYRNAEUS, *Posthomerica*, trans. A. S. Way as *The Fall of Troy*, Loeb Classical Library, vol. 19, London 1913. Quintus repeatedly mentions the Horae in connection with Eos, describing, for example, how *'Dawn [descends] from Olympus' crest of adamant, Dawn, heart-exultant in her radiant steeds amidst the bright-haired Hours'* (ibid.). Aldus Manutius published the *editio princeps* of the epic in Venice in 1504 under the title *Quinti Calabri derelictorum ab Homero libri XIV*. The name Quintus Smyrnaeus was unknown to Manutius, who based his edition on a manuscript discovered by Cardinal Bessarion in Calabria. REBECCHINI, op. cit. (note 24), p. 40, interprets entry no. 189 ('La Ylyada et Odisea di Homero') in inventory no. II of Castiglione's possessions as a referring to a copy of Manutius' publication.

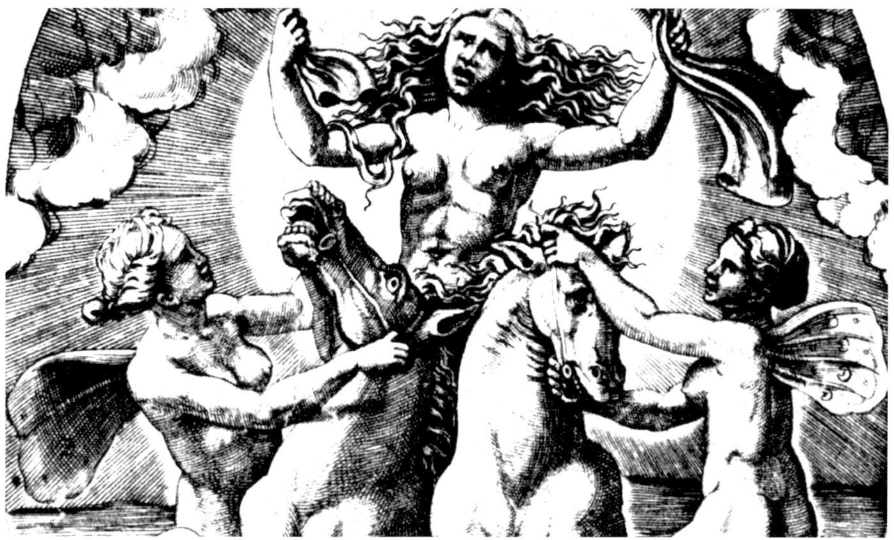

7   Marcantonio Raimondi, detail from the *Aurora*, etching, 17 x 13,3 cm.

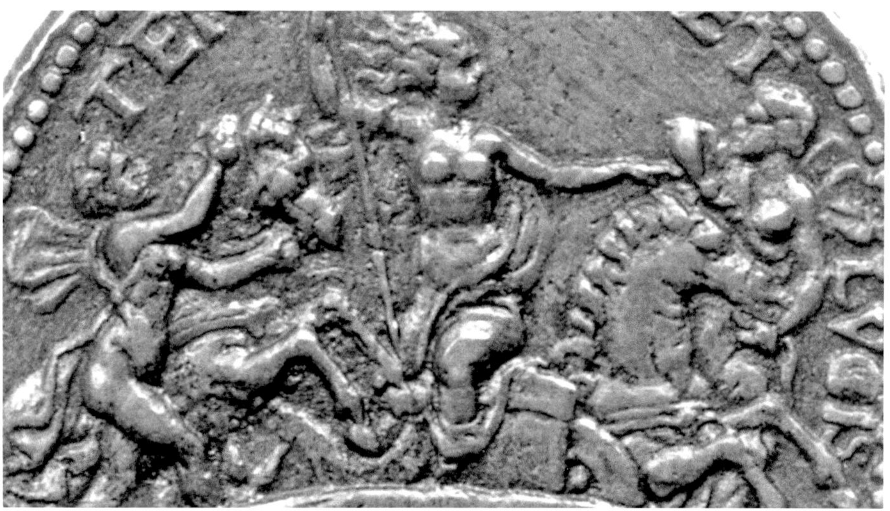

8   Anonymous, detail from the *Aurora*, revers of medal, diameter 3,7 cm.

Raphael painted the portrait of Tebaldeo around the same time as that of Castiglione (fig. 9). Like many humanists, the sitter, Antonio Tebaldi, latinised his name. Born in Ferrara in 1456 or 1463, he trained as a physician (*medico*) and, after pursuing humanist studies, became a tutor at the court of Isabella d'Este. Subsequently called to Mantua by Francesco Gonzaga, he later returned to Ferrara as secretary to Lucrezia Borgia, wife of Alfonso I d'Este. At this time he will have made the acquaintance of such major figures as Pietro Bembo und Lodovico Ariosto. In 1513 he moved to Rome, where he gained the favour of Pope Leo X. According to a contemporary chronicler, Paolo Giovio, he died there in 1535.[38] As Tebaldeo seems to have played no part in the court of Pope Julius II, Giorgio Vasari's statement in his *Vite* that Raphael included Tebaldeo's portrait in the *Parnassus* fresco in the Stanza della Segnatura should be treated with considerable caution.[39] Vasari will have been familiar with Tebaldeo as a writer, not least because he seems to have composed an epitaph for Raphael: Vasari may therefore have accorded him a place in *Parnassus* with no basis in historical fact.[40]

---

38 GINO DE LISA, *Un rimatore cortigiano del Quattrocento*, Salerno 1928, pp. 9f., provides a very brief and not wholly consistent account of Tebaldeo's life. See also NADIA CANNTANA, 'Nuovi elementi per la biografia di Antonio Tebaldeo', in: *The Italianist*, vol. 13, 1993, pp. 47–56, who cites the date of death given by Paolo Giovio but fails to mention Tebaldeo's move to Rome.

39 '*Nella facciata, dunque, di verso Belvedere, dove è il monte Parnaso ed il fonte di Elicona....Sonvi ritratti di naturale tutti i più famosi ed antichi e moderni poeti che si veggono sparsi per il monte....Evvi la dotta Safo e il divinissimo Dante, il leggiadro Petraca e lo amoroso Boccaccio, che vivi vivi sono; il Tibaldeo similmente, ed infiniti altri moderni.*' GIORGIO VASARI, *Vite de' più eccellenti pittori, scultori et architettori* [1568], ed. GAETANO MILANESI, Florence 1906, vol. 4, pp. 334f. For a discussion of which figure in Parnassus might represent Tebaldeo, see DOMINIQUE CORDELLIER and BERNADETTE PY, *Raphaël, son atelier, ses copistes*, Paris 1992, pp. 127f., which lists the proposed identifications.

40 It is as well here to recall the account of Vasari's writing given by BAROLSKY, op. cit. (note 14).

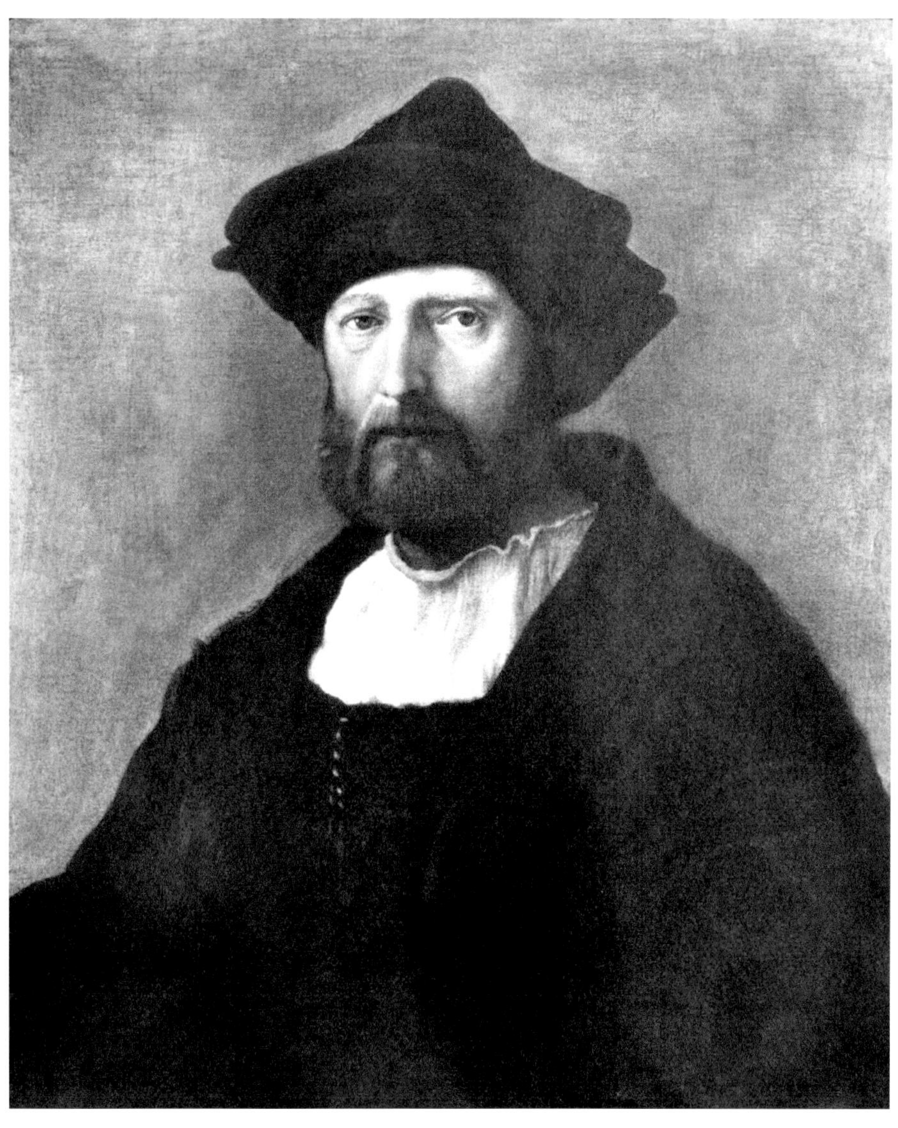

9   Raphael (or copy after), *Portrait of Antonio Tebaldeo*, canvas (?), 84 x 64 cm,
Whereabouts unknown.

In a letter of 19 April 1516 to Bibbiena, Bembo wrote that comparison of the likenesses offered by the portraits of Castiglione and Tebaldeo suggested that the former was by a pupil of Raphael.[41] In the same letter Bembo mentions another portrait associated with Raphael, that of Giuliano de' Medici, but this is of no concern in the present context.[42] This negative appraisal by Bembo, who, like Bibbiena, was friends with Raphael, has caused consternation among scholars. In view of the fine quality of the Louvre canvas it does indeed come as a surprise, even though Bembo – again like Bibbiena – is known to have had a sharp tongue. As regards the Tebaldeo portrait, present-day judges have only an old black and white photograph to go on, and it is not even clear whether this reproduces the original or a very good copy.[43] The present author imagines that Bembo, though he expressly complains about the likeness in the Castiglione portrait, was less displeased by a lack of *similtudo* than by the elaborate conception of an image that shows the sitter as the ideal *cortegiano*. With his humanist learning, Bembo will easily have deciphered the references to the sitter's *virtutes*. And he was surely familiar with the passage from Cicero quoted above, which outlines the essentially classical conception of the portrait.[44] Furthermore, conversations with Castiglione

---

41 *'Il ritratto di M. Baldassar Castiglione, o quello della buona e da me sempre honorata memoria del S. Duca nostro, a cui doni Dio beatitudine, parebbono di mano d'uno de' garzoni di Raphaello, in quanto appartiene al rassomigliarsi, a comperatione di questo Thebaldeo. Io gli ho una grande invidia, chè penso di farmi ritrarre ancho io un giorno'.* Quoted in SHEARMAN, op. cit. (note 13), p. 240.

42 For this portrait, see JÜRG MEYER ZUR CAPELLEN, *Raphael: The Paintings*, vol. 3: *The Roman Portraits, ca. 1508–1520*, Landshut 2008, pp. 183–188.

43 See MEYER ZUR CAPELLEN, op. cit. (note 42), pp. 127–129. REDIG DE CAMPOS ('Dei ritratti di Antonio Tebaldeo e di altri nel Parnaso di Raffaello', in: *Archivio della Società romana di Storia patria*, 3rd ser., vol. 6, 1952, pp. 51–58) and LUITPOLD DUSSLER (*Raphael*, London 1971, p. 43) give different locations for the painting.

44 Bembo was undoubtedly well-versed in the writings of classical antiquity and will have been particularly familiar with the works of Cicero. The same applies to Castiglione, whose possessions included a number of editions of Cicero. See REBECCHINI, op. cit. (note 24), pp. 30-44.

will have acquainted Bembo with the basic tenets of *Il libro del cortegiano* and, in addition, he was among the first to receive the second, revised manuscript, in May 1518.[45] He also maintained close relations with Raphael. Friends at the papal court were, of course, rivals as well. In view of this, the remarks in Bembo's letter are possibly best interpreted as a fit of pique. Perhaps understandably, he will not have taken kindly to seeing his friend depicted as a paragon of a courtier, not least since he urgently desired Raphael to paint his own portrait.[46]

Tebaldeo, too, belonged to Raphael's circle of friends, and Bembo's letter is an important piece of documentary evidence relating to this painting. The viewpoint is comparable to that in the Castiglione portrait and the composition vaguely similar (figs. 1, 9). However, Tebaldeo is dressed more plainly than Castiglione. Over a pleated white shirt he wears a doublet buttoned up at the chest; a fur garment is draped around his shoulders. His beard is trimmed, unlike Castiglione's, and he sports a wide *biretta*. In contrast to Castiglione's, Tebaldeo's attire does not depart from current norms: closely related clothing occurs in a number of roughly contemporaneous portraits by Sebastiano del Piombo, and Raphael himself is very similarly dressed in his well-known *Double Portrait* in the Louvre.[47] Tebaldeo's costume places the painting firmly in the period under discussion here and shows the sitter attired in a distinguished, but by no means extravagant, manner. Comparison of the two portraits further reveals a very different gaze in each case. Tebaldeo fixes the viewer with a determined look, its almost fierce energy coming across even in the old photograph. The composition underscores this central feature of the portrait and focuses attention on its expressive force. Tebaldeo's intense gaze doubtless symbolises his intellectual powers, and this may have been what Bembo was referring to obliquely in his letter when mentioning the

---

45 Ludovico Canossa conveyed this version of *Il cortegiano* to Bembo and to Sadoleto. See BARBERIS, op. cit. (note 1), p. LXXXIII.
46 See note 41.
47 See MEYER ZUR CAPELLEN, op. cit. (note 42), pp. 136–143.

portrait's 'likeness'. Yet Raphael's image also embodies a *virtus* of major significance to men of letters, using the clothing to point to the sitter's essential humility in the context of a monumental composition that hones in on the face and its expressive qualities.

Tebaldeo paid tribute to Raphael's portrait of him in a sonnet.[48] In the way of humanists, he invoked artists of classical antiquity, Apelles and Zeuxis, to give a suitably lofty aura to his thanks for the gift embodied in Raphael's portrait. For present-day viewers, the artistic quality of the image, and the sense of mental energy emanating from it, are perhaps more vividly conveyed by a rather lustreless copy now in the Uffizi in Florence, which bears an inscription identifying the sitter by name (fig. 10).[49]

Raphael's portraits of Castiglione and Tebaldeo form an intriguing pair of opposites. The image of Castiglione can be read as a piece of finely composed poetry in paint. Although the quality of the painting as such is immediately apparent, for a full understanding the viewer requires a humanist's knowledge. Contemporaries equipped with such knowledge might see themselves as the sitter's equal, deriving both pleasure and confirmation of their own learning from con-

---

48 See SHEARMAN, op. cit. (note 13), pp. 277f.: *'Se nel scriver a me fosse concessa / La excellenza che a voi ne la pittura, / Non, Raphael, da me vostra figura / Men che da voi la mia vedreste expressa, / Ma più vivace assai perché è sommessa, / Vostra arte a gli anni; vive la scrittura / Di tanti antichi ancor: qual opra dura / Di Zeusi o Apelle? Ognuna ha il tempo oppressa. / Ma raro è chi ben scriva, e resta extinto, / Se chiaro inchiostro no ,l consacra e honora, / Il descritto più presto assai che il pinto. / Pur io dirò viva il mio verso o mora, / che un in pinger sol avere vinto / La man di Zeusi, ma in donar anchora.'* Without committing himself, Shearman notes briefly that Tebaldeo arrived in Rome either in 1513 or at the end of 1515. On the issue of whether Bembo or Tebaldeo wrote the epitaph for Raphael in the Pantheon, see ibid., pp. 640–647.

49 The copy, painted by Stefano dell' Altissimo, forms part of the Uffizi portrait gallery. See LUCIANO BERTI, ed., *Gli Uffizi: Catalogo generale*, Florence 1970, no. Ic 112, p. 617.

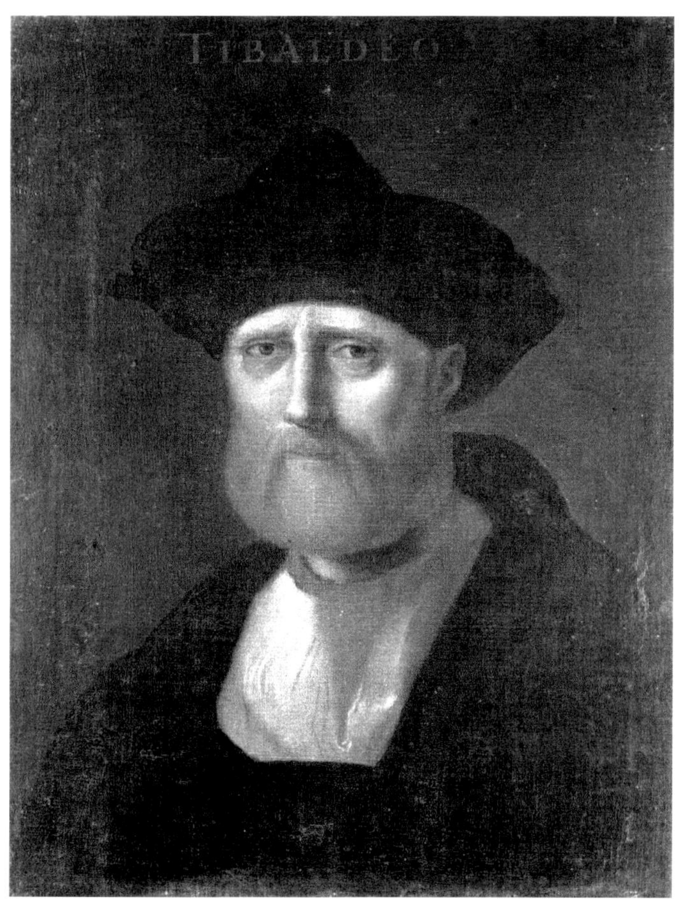

10   Raphael, copy after,
*Portrait of
Antonio Tebaldeo*,
Florence, Uffizi,
Portrait Gallery.

templation of the portrait. Yet the painting could also have the opposite effect, as Bembo's reaction shows. The portrait of Tebaldeo, by contrast, possesses an immediacy that seems to acquaint the viewer directly with the sitter's personality. It is tempting to echo Cicero's judgement that *'all depends upon the face, and the power of the face is centred in the eyes'*, but to realise this it is not necessary to have read Cicero.

This article is devoted to Joachim Poeschke and will be published in the German language in the volume Virtus in Kunst und Kunsttheorie der italienischen Renaissance, *ed.* THOMAS WEIGEL *and* BRITTA KUSCH-ARNHOLD, *Münster 2011.*

Studies on
the MADONNA DELL'IMPANNATA

The following studies concentrate on Raphael's invention of the *Madonna dell'Impannata,* which has been handed down to us in some different an interesting versions. The most famous is the painting in the Galleria Palatina in Florence, whose authorship for a long time was discussed controversially, sometime denying the execution by Raphael himself. Today there is only little doubt on his immediate participation, but usually one admits his collaboration with the workshop. Recently there has surfaced a version coming from the Northwick Collection and up to now unknown in the literature relevant to the subject. This painting is of high painterly quality and so this study will be focussed on it. The third version is that in Corsham Court, which in the 19th belonged to Reverend John Sanford. By him it was introduced to the public as the real original done by Raphael himself disqualifying the version in the Galleria Palatina. Sanford's painting was debated in the 19th century, but today generally is regarded as a copy. James Methuen-Campbell, the present owner of the picture, allowed to do some photographs, which allow a new look upon this paintings, which too has to be discussed briefly. Claudio Falcucci made some colour photographs and some infra-red reflectographs of the *Madonna dell' Impannata* at Corsham Court and contributed a technological report on the *Madonna dell'Impannata Northwick.*

I.   The MADONNA DELL'IMPANNATA NORTHWICK

Provenance

The painting of a *Madonna dell'Impannata* which recently surfaced in Italian private ownership and is here to be discussed, descends from the Northwick Collection in Thirlestane House in Cheltenham (plate I, fig. 1). This situation is documented by a *cartellino* which is still found today on the back of the painting (fig. 2). This information is strengthened furthermore by a passage in the sale catalogue of the Northwick Collection of 1859.[1] Number 1601 has an entry reading: '*RAFFAELLE (SCHOOL). La Madonna dell'Impannata. From the collection of the Rev. J. Sanford, who bought it from Florence in the year 1838.*' (fig. 3) The reference about the origin of the painting as in the Sanford Collection at first appears irritating, as the Reverend Sanford owned a painting of the *Madonna dell'Impannata* which he believed to be the original (see chapter II), whereas the version then in the Galleria Palatina in Florence, which is today unanimously given to Raphael, the Reverend took for a copy. The painting from the Northwick Collection however, is undoubtedly a finished work. Now the entry in the sale catalogue of the Northwick Collection of 1859 allows only two interpretations. It is either a mistaken statement about the provenance of a picture Sanford bought some twenty years earlier or the Reverend bought a second version of the *Madonna dell'Impannata* to remove from the market a rival to his highly treasured "original".[2] This would mean that Sanford at an unknown date sold the

---

1   *Catalogue of the Late Lord Northwick's Extensive and Magnificent Collection of Ancient and Modern Pictures, ... at Thirlstane House, Cheltenham. Which will be sold by auction by* MR. PHILIPPS *at the Mansion, On Tuesday, the 20th of July, 1859, ...* One copy of this sale catalogue can be found in the Holbourne Museum of Art in Bath.

2   Such a procedure is not unusual among collectors and dealers. In Sanford's account book for 1838 no acquisition is recorded of a *Madonna dell'Impannata.* This may imply that he acquired the picture in question en bloc with others, or thought it unnecessary or not sensible to make a note of the acquisition of a further version.

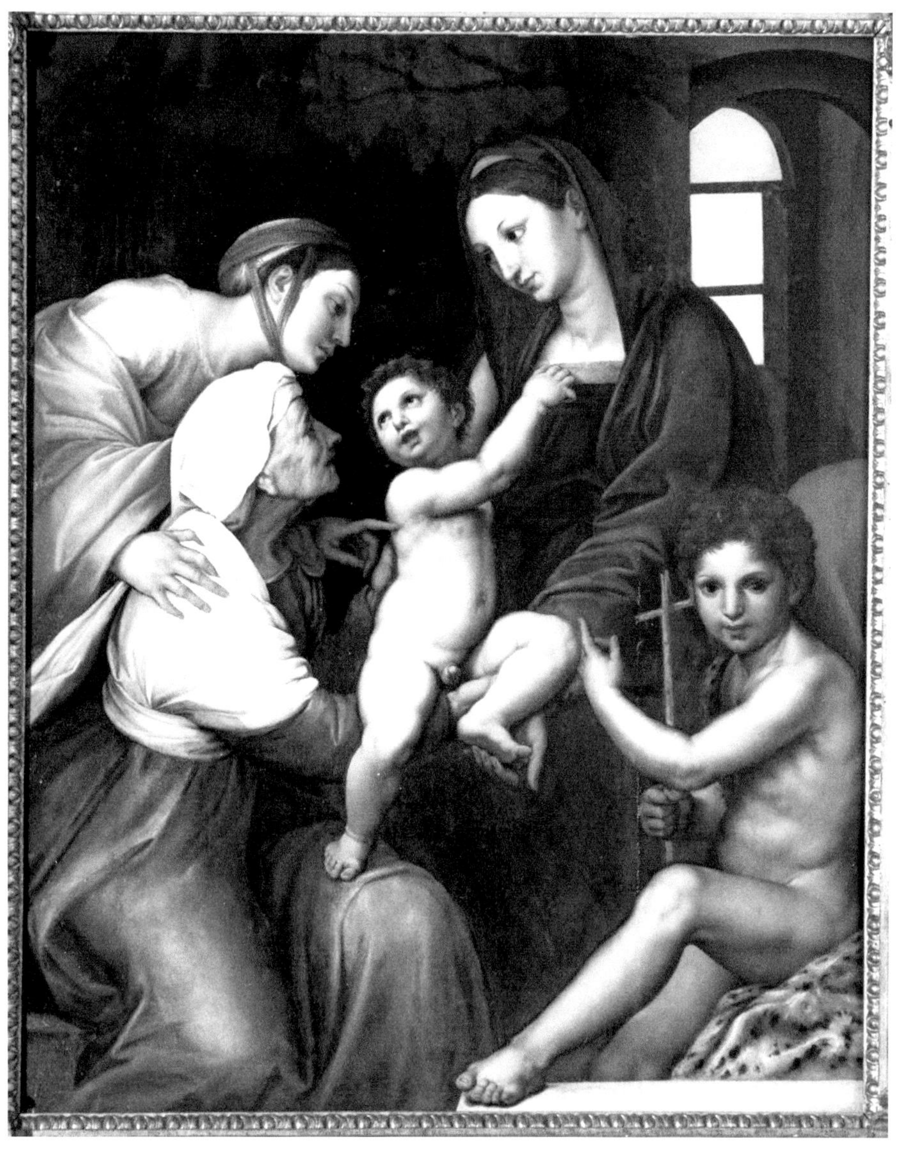

1   *Madonna dell'Impannata Northwick*, oil on poplar, 150,8 x 121,3 cm,
private collection.

2   Cartellino on the back side of the *Madonna dell' Impannata Northwick.*

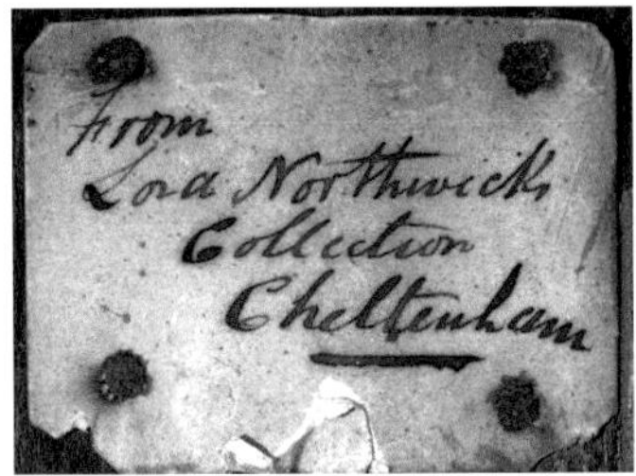

3   Frontispiece of the sale catalogue of the Northwick Collection of 1859.

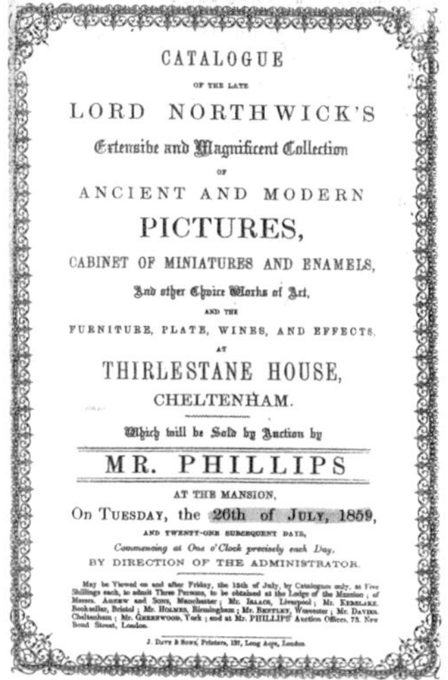

picture aquired in 1838 to Lord Northwick. After the Lord's decease the painting was sold at the above-mentioned auction.[3] So far it is not known who bought it at the auction, the painting returned in the twentieth century to Italy and there was acquired by the present owner.

Condition, Technological Examination, and Quality of the Picture

The painting of the *Madonna dell'Impannata Northwick* has an eighteenth century frame in classical Renaissance style (plate III). As it is nowhere cut back we may assume that the frame was made specifically for this painting. According to the *Archivio Storico Araldico Italiano*, the badge recognizable on the frame is rather late and unspecific and would hardly be identifiable (fig. 4). So far no early depiction of the painting in this frame has been found which might enable us to identify the provenance with greater precision.[4]

---

3   GUSTAV WAAGEN, *Galleries and Cabinets of Art in Great Britain ...*, *Forming a Supplement Volume to the Treasures of Art in Great Britain*, London 1867, reprint Elibron Classics, London 2003, vol. 2, pp. 195-212. Waagen only had one day to see the 800 paintings at Thirlestaine House in Cheltenham. He does not mention the *Madonna dell'Impannata* – perhaps because it was filed as a copy.

4   For example the Northwick Collection, of which various gallery paintings have survived; see OLIVER BRADBURY and NICHOLAS PENNY. 'The picture collecting of Lord Northwick', in: *The Burlington Magazine*, CXLIV, 2002, part I, pp. 485-496; part II, pp. 606-617.

The painting from the Northwick Collection (plate I) with its measurements of 150,8 x 121,3 cm is only slightly smaller than the measurements of about 160 x 126 cm of the picture in the Galleria Palatina.[5] This means that the composition of the Northwick version was clearly cut back in height and almost invisibly along the border. Hence it would have been possible to reuse for the execution of this painting preparatory studies (presumably a cartoon) done for the picture of the Galleria Palatina.

In 1992 the picture was restored by the workshop Nicola Restauri in Aramengo near Turin. Firstly the damage to the support was repaired which consisted of four panels made of poplar wood. They were strengthened and the two battens renewed. (plate II). Then the much yellowed varnish was removed (see Appendix I). The condition of the varnish suggests that it was applied only after a cleaning of the picture in the nineteenth century.

The present overall condition (plates IV–X) can be called excellent for a painting dating from the sixteenth century. However, Maria's mantle has suffered due to an application of a layer of ultramarine over a layer of *smalt* which in the course of time partly suffered.[6] The colours of the painting were applied boldly with thin layers of paint. This would indicate that the painterly execution took a relatively short time in comparison to that of the version in the Gallerina Palatina. In less important parts like those

4   The *Madonna dell'Impannata Northwick*, detail of the frame.

---

5   For the condition of this painting see RAFFAELLO NARDI BERTI et al. in: MINA GREGORI et al., *Raffaello a Firenze: Dipinti e disegni delle collezioni florentine*, Florence 1984, pp. 265-267. There in connection with the restoration of the picture its condition and the results of the X-ray photographs as well as of the infra-red reflectographs are discussed.

6   This technical method has been known since the fifteenth century. For documentation about the procedure see the record by CLAUDIO FALCUCCI of 19 April 2010 (Appendix II), which complements the examination by the NICOLA workshop.

rather quickly executed costume areas hair craquelure is evident, while the flesh tones especially on faces have a much more solid paint consistency and therefore less craquelure. In the sixteenth century these features are classical differentiations and can also be found repeatedly in Raphael's œuvre.

In general the painterly quality is extremely high. The execution of the four heads arranged in the ideal centre of the picture captivates with its delicate, meticulously applied modelling and the contrasting faces of different ages. In the fine characterization of Saint Anne's profile as well as in the execution of the young faces of Mary and the female Saint on the left we can see quality as well as a painterly handwriting which is very close to the picture in the painting at the Galleria Palatina. The garments seem to have been applied somewhat faster, for instance the one Saint Anne is wearing. The execution of the young Saint John is particulary interesting with his body seemingly slightly less sturdily modelled than that in the picture at the Galleria Palatina. The execution of the leopard's hide is indeed very daring, and here appears even more alive. The painting was studied by the experts Mina Gregori and Dianne Dwyer Modestini in 2007 resp. 2008, who confirmed the high quality of the painting.[7]

In 2007 and 2008 the Nicola Restauri workshop carried out the technological examination of the *Madonna dell'Impannata Northwick* (see Appendix I). This established that the painting contained no pigments which were used only after the sixteenth century. This is actually already enough to rule out that we are dealing with a later copy.[8] Of particular interest are the

---

7   DIANNE DWYER MODESTINI resumed her examination of the painting: *'In my opinion the ex Corsham painting of the 'Madonna dell'Impannata' is a replica from the bottega of Raphael, close, both in period and authorship to the painting in the Galleria Palatina, which must, however, be the first version, …'* MINA GREGORI stated: *'Alla luce di tutte queste considerazioni ritengo che la tavola già a Corsham Court sia opera della bottega di Raffaello.'* Both scholars were not aware the fact that the *Madonna dell'Impannata Northwick* though descending from the Sanford Collection never entered Corsham Court. Their expertises are kept by the present owner of the painting.

8   The complete records are kept by the present owner of the painting.

X-ray photographs and the infra-red reflectographs. The X-ray photograph of the whole picture (fig. 5) shows up very clearly a refined application of lead white which is very close to Raphael's method.[9] This feature is especially obvious in the modelling of the bodies as well as in the drapery. Furthermore the complete X-ray photograph shows that for this version originally no inside architecture like that in the Galleria Palatina was intended, but instead a background landscape which has partially reappeared in the upper part. The scenic view on the right shows a mighty tree which stretches out a powerful branch to the left – as if crowning the central group of figures. The probably first draft, which differed from the original version was rejected however, and overpainted again along the lines of the earlier composition.[10] Such changes of the background do appear occasionally in Raphael's work and can indeed be taken as a characteristic of his artistic procedure.[11] In the case of the *Madonna dell'Impannata Northwick* this means that at first a variant was planned.

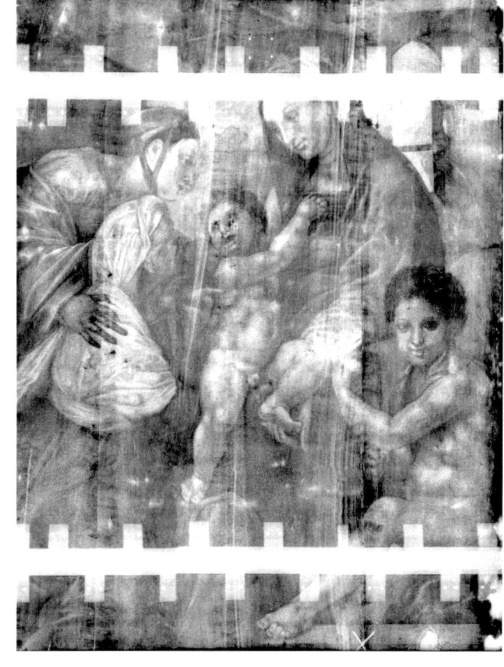

5
Madonna dell'Impannata Northwick,
X-ray (Nicola).

---

9   See the poor X-ray photograph of the painting in the Galleria Palatina which is difficult to read (fig. 15).

10 The underpaintings are recognizable even with the naked eye; they are particularly distinct in the photographs taken with raking light. When the overpainting was applied, however, the lattice-work of the *panni* in the window was waived – so here white areas appear.

11 In this context we may refer to the *Bridgewater Madonna*. In this case the original landscape vistas were later overpainted; see JÜRG MEYER ZUR CAPELLEN, *Raphael. A Critical Catalogue of His Paintings*, vol. 1: *The Beginnings in Umbria and Florence ca. 1500–1508*, Landshut 2001, no. 24, pp. 206-210 and no. 33, pp. 250-253.

The infra-red reflectographs (see Appendix I) uniformly show light outer contours to which are added in particular indications of drapery and in the area of the faces also inner outlines (for example the eyes, noses, mouths and ears). It is striking that these contours during the execution of the picture were lightly corrected several times. The contours show no *spolveri*, but we can assume that the executing artist transferred the established cartoon by indentation. The more important drawings were applied with a lighter touch, but they have to be distinguished from those with a shaky line, which obviously followed a model and thus can be classified as indentations (fig. 6). Saint Anne's profile is a characteristic example of this drawing manner.[12] – Another interesting feature is the depiction of the eyes. The underdrawings of the pupil regularly show two concentric circles. The pupil looks like a black space, while the iris is brighter and enclosed by an boldly drawn circle. This feature seems to be a regular procedure of

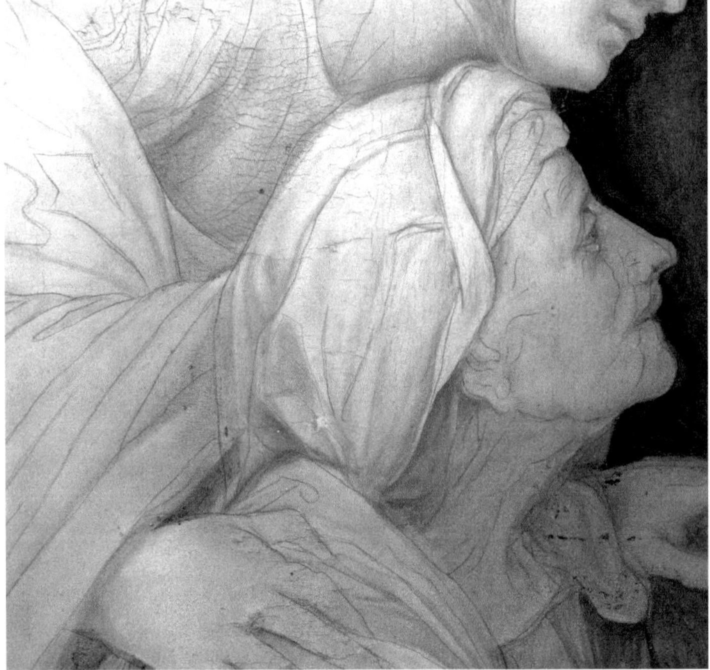

6 *Madonna dell' Impannata Northwick*, infra-red reflectography, detail (Falcucci).

---

12 For the identification of this figure as St. Anne see MEYER ZUR CAPELLEN, op. cit. (note 11), p. 146.

Raphael's.[13] In the *Madonna dell'Impannata Northwick* the painterly execution of the pupils are sometimes fully blacked and in relation to the preparatory drawing occasionally also slightly shifted, as one can recognize for instance on the face of the young Saint John (Appendix I).[14]

The actual technical investigation, done in 2010 by Claudio Falcucci, allow further differentiations. His new infra-red reflectographs demonstrate more clearly between the underlying drawings and the final execution. The striking reflectography, taken from the head of Saint Anne shows two different line – one a little shaky, the other done more fluently. This aspect confirms the supposition that the cartoon was transferred by indentation. To summarize we can draw attention to the fact that the underdrawings are applied with determination and gusto; in some areas smaller *pentimenti* can be made out. The shaky preparatory drawings allow the assumption that a cartoon was used. It is very likely that the underdrawings are the work of Raphael's assistants.[15] It has to be pointed out that during

---

13 See for example the infra-red reflectographs in MAURIZIO SARACENI, 'Il disegno sottostante nella pittura di Raffaello', in: *Raffaello e l'idea della bellezza*, ed. ALESSANDRO VEZZOSI, vol. 3, Perugia 2001. The procedure is particularly clear to be seen in the so-called *Muta*, ibid., p. 30.

14 This procedure is similar to that found in the eyes of the young Saint John in the painting in the Galleria Palatina in so far that one blackened pupil is almost completely hidden by the underpainting; see NARDI BERTI in GREGORI 1984, op. cit (note 5), p. 44. So far no further infra-red reflectographs of the painting in the Galleria Palatina have been published which could test this aspect more closely.

15 We can hardly make Raphael responsible for the underdrawing. If one compares for example the Madonna's head in the underdrawing of the *Madonna dell'Impannata Northwick* with that of the *Aldobrandini Madonna* at the London National Gallery, the performance of the hand shows obvious differences. We can assume that the underdrawing of the *Aldobrandini Madonna* was executed by Raphael himself on the basis of an axle cross and mainly applied freehand. The delicacy and artistic riches of this underdrawing are shown by the assured grasp of the outlines, the occasional exploring lines and the light shadings suggesting shadows – everything is of a high quality and indeed characteristic of the artist's drawing practice; see also MEYER ZUR CAPELLEN, op. cit. (note 11), no. 48, pp. 71ff. For details see also JILL DUNKERTON

Raphael's advanced Roman period preparatory work like the production of cartoons or compositions to be realized were left increasingly to assistants.[16] It is possible furthermore to document the close cooperation of Raphael and with his assistants, in later works especially with Giulio Romano.[17]

In the present case however, the quality of the execution of the faces and the flesh tones in general would suggest that Raphael himself intimately supervised the process. The somewhat stronger modelling of the young Saint John as well as the brilliant realization the leopard's hide immediately makes one think of Giulio Romano's involvement. On account of the overall qualities mentioned earlier I am in no doubt that the picture was created in Raphael's workshop. The *Madonna dell'Impannata Northwick* is highly significant for our understanding of the practices and methods in Raphael's workshop. Future studies in this field hopefully will allow a better understanding of the whole complex.

II. The MADONNA DELL'IMPANNATA at Corsham Court

A painting now at Corsham Court is closely related to the *Madonna dell'Impannata Northwick* (plate XI). The Corsham picture was acquired in the nineteenth century by the Reverend John Sanford, who entered it in his account book as *'bought by Rev. John Sanford in Florence 7th March 1834 from casa Rivani. He paid 1500 pauli for it. He bought it as a copy by Giulio Romano.'*[18] In 1845 Sanford published a

---

and NICHOLAS PENNY, 'The Infra-Red Examination of Raphael's Gavargh Madonna', in: *National Gallery Technical Bulletin*, vol. 14, 1993, pp. 7-21.

16 For example the cartoon for the *Madonna del Divin Amore* in Naples, Museo Capodimonte; see MEYER ZUR CAPELLEN, op. cit. (note 11), no. A8, pp. 247-251.

17 For example the *Holy Family* at the Prado, the so-called *La Perla*, see MEYER ZUR CAPELLEN, op. cit. (note 11), no. 64, pp. 183-189.

18 John Sanford's account book is housed in the Barber Institute of Fine Arts in Birmingham. James Methuen-Campbell very kindly allowed me to consult his copy of the original. The *paolo* was a Florentine unit of currency, containing about 45 grams of fine

booklet recording the views of experts who considered his painting to be Raphael's original.[19] It has occasionally been conjectured that the picture listed in Sanford's account book is identical with that in the Northwick Collection, but this cannot be the case because, in accordance with succession law, the painting was transferred from the Sanford Collection directly to Corsham Court, where it can still be seen in the Cabinet Room (fig. 7).[20] With the kind permission of James Methuen-Campbell it has been possible to study the picture closely in this room, where Claudio Falcucci was allowed to take colour photographs of it and produce infrared reflectographs.

Nineteenth-century commentators noted that the painting was unfinished and that Raphael's underdrawing was clearly visible. Both of these aspects can be seen with the naked eye. The incompleteness is particularly obvious in the area of St John's head and upper body (fig. 8), where in several places the surface of the painting consists of nothing more than

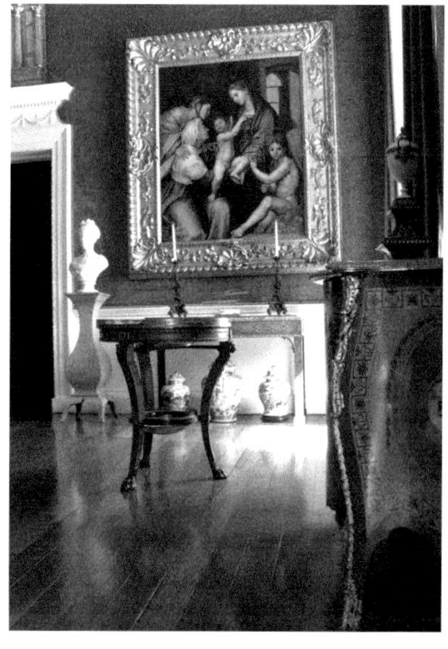

7 *Madonna dell'Impannata,* Corsham Court.

---

silver, in widespread use in the Grand Duchy of Tuscany in the eighteenth and nineteenth centuries. See Richard Klimpert, *Lexikon der Münzen, Maße und Gewichte, Zählarten und Zeitgrößen aller Länder der Erde,* Berlin 1896, reprint Graz 1972, p. 262.

19 *The History of the Picture called the Madonna dell'Impannata in the Possession of the Rev. John Sanford,* London, n.d. (c. 1845). See also page 2.

20 See Waagen, op. cit. (note 2), vol. 2, no. 23, p. 397 and Benedict Nicholson, 'The Sanford Collection', in: *The Burlington Magazine,* XCVII, 1973, pp. 207-214. Borenius described the picture in situ in his catalogue of the Corsham Court Collection. Tancred Borenius, *A Catalogue of the Pictures at Corsham Court,* London 1939, no. 69, pp. 36f.

underpainting. In contrast, other sections, including the central area with the four heads, appear largely finished (fig. 9).[21]

The extensive drawing visible in the Corsham picture varies in character. A delicate underdrawing it is notably clear in the outlines of Christ's left leg (fig. 10). Elsewhere, for example in the Virgin's hand supporting Christ's leg, especially in the fingernails, it takes the form of broader brushstrokes. That is also how it appears in the hand of the standing female saint, which shows heavily retraced lines (fig. 11). The drawing of this hand appears crude when compared with that in the preparatory study now in Berlin, which also exhibits some retracing (fig. 17).[22] In fact, the bolder brush drawing in the painting must be attributed to a different artist. Moreover, it would seem to have been added at a considerably later date.

The figure of the Madonna is particularly problematic. Her brilliant blue drapery appears especially fine when the painting is viewed hanging on the wall (plate XI, fig. 7). Yet infra-red reflectography reveals that this area must be of considerably later date (fig. 12). Whereas the Virgin's head was executed on the basis of underdrawing, her garment was laid in with boldly brushed underpainting. Unknown in Raphael's day, this technical procedure may point to an origin in the nineteenth century. It can be assumed that the broader brush drawing, too, formed part of this later intervention.

The photographs taken by Claudio Falcucci in the Cabinet Room at Corsham Court inevitably lack the high degree of precision obtainable in a studio, but they do reveal some delicate, finely executed preliminary drawing. That of St John's face, for instance, certainly approaches the quality of the underdrawing in the *Madonna dell'Impannata Northwick* (fig. 13). This suggests that the Corsham Court canvas, too, was

---

21 However, close inspection also reveals extensive drawing here, notably in St Anne's head. As noted below, the drawing would seem to date from a later period.

22 Some scholars doubt whether the retracings in the Berlin drawing are by Raphael. Paul Joannides, *The Drawings of Raphael, with a Complete Catalogue*, Oxford 1983, no. 326, p. 214, for instance, suggests they date from a slightly later period.

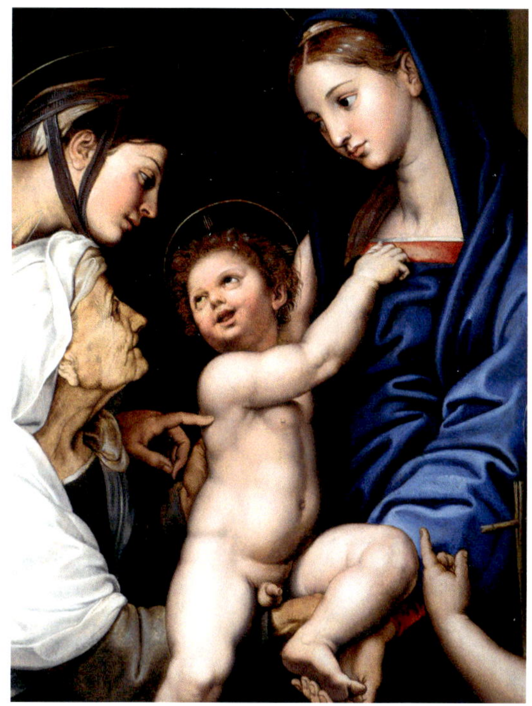

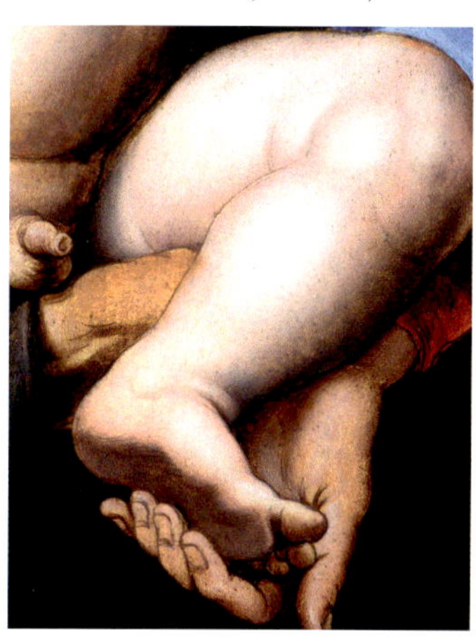

8–11
Details of the
Madonna dell'Impannata,
Corsham Court (Falcucci).

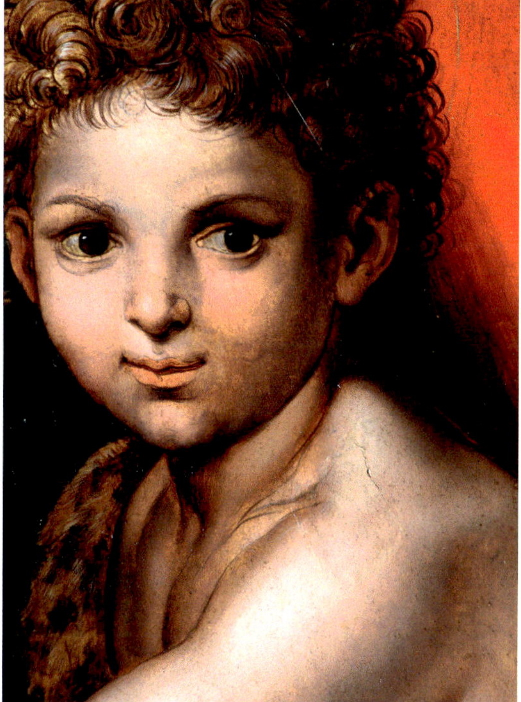

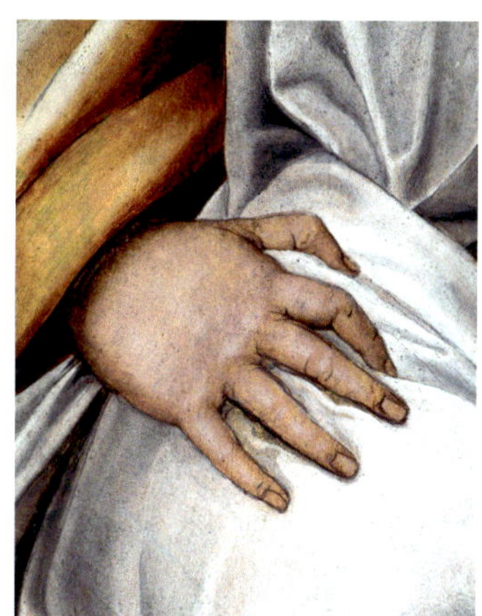

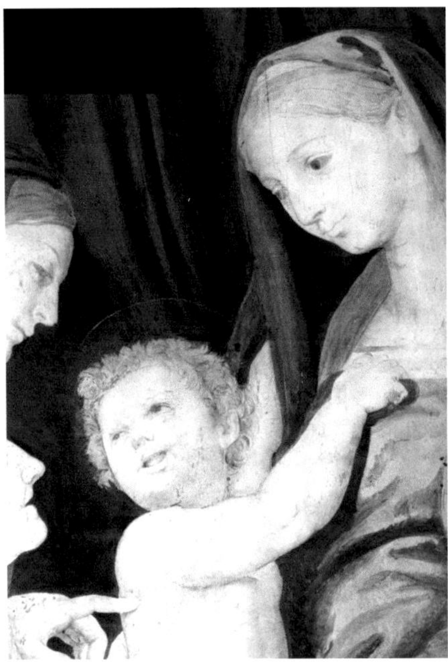

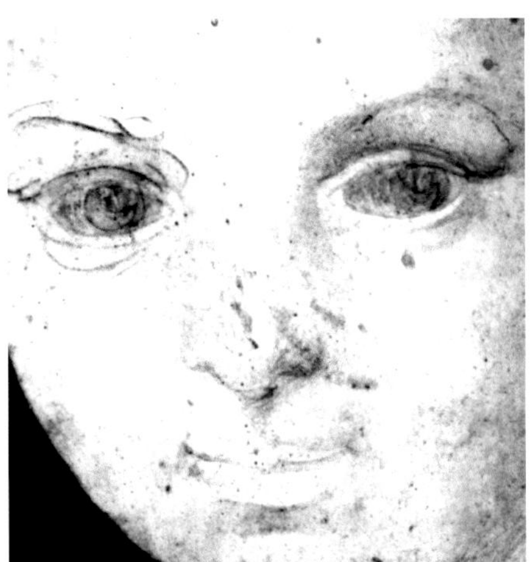

12 and 13
*Madonna dell'Impannata,*Corsham Court,
infra-red reflectography, details, (Falcucci).

produced in Raphael's workshop, but not completed until the nineteenth century. Further examination of the painting in the future would hopefully shed more light on it.

III. The Madonna dell'Impannata of the Galleria Palatina and Problems of Raphael's Workshop

In his *Life of Raphael* (1568), Giorgio Vasari mentioned that the Florentine banker Bindo Altoviti (1491-1557) commissioned a painting known as the *Madonna dell'Impannata*[23] and at an early but unknown date moved it to the family's estate in Florence (fig. 14). After his participation in an abortive coup in 1554, Cosimo I de' Medici confiscated Altoviti's Florentine estates and installed the *Madonna dell'Impannata* as an altarpiece in his own palace chapel.[24] In

____

23 Florence, Galleria Palatina, Panel, 160 x 126 cm, inv. 1912, no. 94.

24 See GIORGIO VASARI, *Le vite de' più eccellenti architetti, pittori e scultori italiani*, Florence 1568, ed. GAETANO MILANESI, 8 vols., 1906, reprint Florence 1981, vol. 4, pp. 351f. *'... e similmente un quadro di Nostra Donna che egli (Bindo Altoviti) mandò a*

1589 the painting entered the Tribuna of the Uffizi and in 1697 the Palazzo Pitti in Florence. In 1799 under Napoleon the painting was stolen and in 1816 reinstalled at its previous site.[25] Vasari himself already praised the work to the sky, and it was extremely popular and widely appreciated far into the nineteenth century. In modern art criticism, Passavant was the first to question whether Raphael himself had executed the major part of the composition.[26] He was followed by

> *Fiorenza; il qual quadro è oggi nel palazzo della duca Cosimo nella cappella delle stanze nuove e da me fatte e dipinte, e serve per tavola dell'altare; ed in esso è dipinta una Santa Anna vecchissima a sedere, la quale porge alla Nostra Donna il suo Figliuolo di tanta bellezza nell'ignudo e nelle fattezze del volto, che nel suo ridere rallegra chiunque lo guarda: senza che Raffaello mostrò nel dipignere la Nostra Donna tutto quello che di bellezza si può fare nell'aria di una vergine, dove sia accompagnata negli occhi modestia, nella fronte onore, nel naso grazia, e nella bocca virtù; senza che l'abito suo è tale, che mostra una semplicità ed onestà infinita. E nel vero io non penso, che per tanta cosa si possa veder meglio. Evvi un San Giovanni a seder, ignudo; ed un'altra Santa, ch'è bellissima anch'ella. Così per campo vi è un casamento, dove egli ha finto una finestra impannata che fa lume alla stanza, dove le figure son dentro. ...'*. See too RAFFAELLO BORGHINI, *Il Riposo*, 1584. Extract on the life of Raphael in VINCENZO GOLZIO, *Raffaello nei documenti ...*, Città del Vaticano 1936, reprint 1971, pp. 265-269, who mentioned the picture still in the palace chapel of Grand Duke Francesco, devotes to him an extended description. (See JOHN SHEARMAN, *Raphael in Early Modern Sources 1483-1602*, New Haven and London 2003, vol. 2, p. 1326).

25 See in detail ETTORE ALLEGRI in GREGORI 1984, op. cit (note 5), pp. 166-173.

26 It is possible that doubts about the autograph character of the Pitti picture were raised before the suggestion given by JOHANN DAVID PASSAVANT, *Rafael von Urbino und sein Vater Giovanni Santi*, vol. 2, Leipzig 1839, pp. 394f.; vol. 3, Leipzig 1858, pp. 166f. He might have heard some rumours. In the publication *The History of the Picture called the Madonna dell'Impannata in the Possession of the Rev. John Sanford* (ca. 1845, p. 14) – which had a small print run and no indication of an author – a printed letter of 1 January 1843 by GEORGE AUGUSTUS WALLIS appeared where he remarked, *'First, the Picture of the Impannata painted by Raffael for Florence was never finished, as one or two others of that period. The one called Raffael in the Palace Pitti, was sent to Paris, and the whole body of artists declared it NOT TO BE HIS, and could not be placed as such among his other works, and was sent to the Luxembourg as of the school of that Divine Master.'* As far as I know these events do not appear

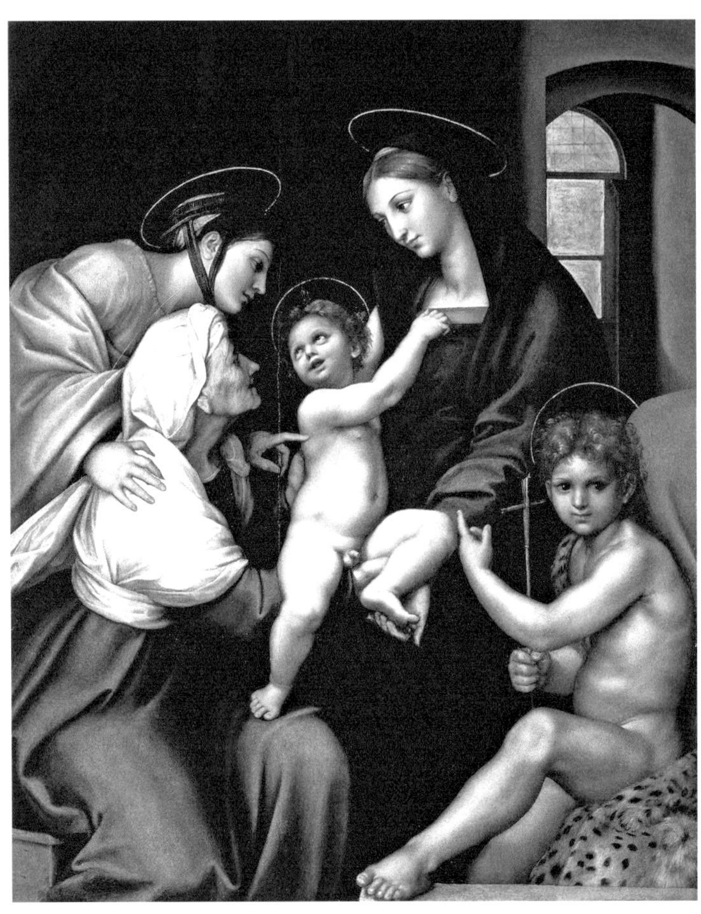

14 *Madonna dell'
Impannata*,
oil on wood,
160 x 126 cm,
Florence,
Galleria Palatina.

other scholars like Crowe and Cavalcaselle, Fischel, Dussler and most recently Brown and Chong.[27]

anywhere in the relevant literature. See ETTORE ALLEGRI in GREGORI 1984, op. cit. (note 5), p. 173, note 36.; the authors too offer the summary of the critical history on p. 168.

27 JOSEPH ARCHER CROWE and GIOVANNI B. CAVALCASELLE, *Raphael: His Life and Works*, London 1885, vol. 2, pp. 170ff.; PIERLUIGI DE VECCHI, *Raffael*, Munich 2002, vol. 2, pp. 170ff.; OSKAR FISCHEL, *Raphael*, London 1948, vol. 1, p. 364; LUITPOLD DUSSLER, *Raphael: A Critical Catalogue of His Pictures, Wall-Paintings and Tapestries*, London and New York 1971, pp. 38f.; ALAN CHONG et al., ed., *Raphael, Cellini and a Renaissance Banker: The Patronage of Bindo Altoviti*, Boston 2003, pp. 380ff.; see also the summary in DOMINIQUE CORDELLIER and BERNADETTE PY, *Raphaël: Son atelier, ses copistes. Musée du Louvre. Inventaire général des dessins italiens*, Paris 1992, p. 198.

On the occasion of the great Raphael exhibition in 1984 the *Madonna dell' Impannata* – now displayed in the Galleria Palatina – was restored and underwent technical examination. The participating scholars concluded that the painting was of high quality and in parts worthy of Raphael. The X-ray photograph furthermore revealed a crucial change of the overall con-

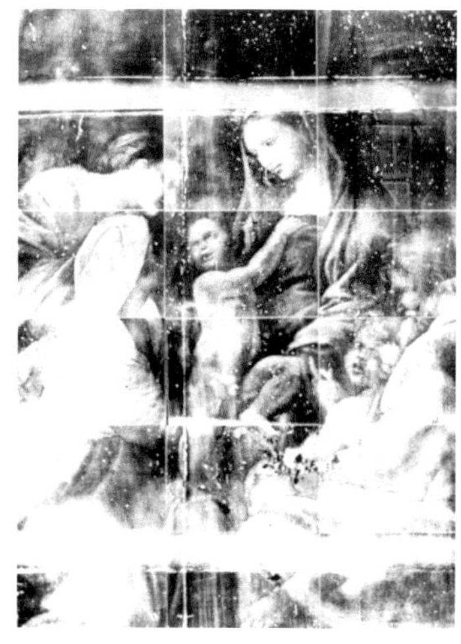

15
Madonna dell' Impannata,
Florence,
Galleria Palatina,
X-ray.

ception: Saint Joseph should have been sitting in the lower right and not the young Saint John as now (fig. 15). This modification of the original conception is documented by two preliminary autograph drawings (figs. 16, 17).[28] Such a situation would suggest that the genesis of the composition took a rather long time. The characteristics of the painting furthermore suggest major participation of the workshop. Contrary to occasional speculation however, it is impossible to identify the hand of any specific assistant. The overall high quality of the painting seems to indicate that the composition was produced immediately under Raphael's supervision and with his personal participation.[29] For a long time the dating of the painting fluctuated between 1511 and 1516. Today a period of about 1513 and 1515 is widely accepted.[30]

---

28 The one in Windsor Castle (inv. RL 12742) only shows the main group and lacks the figure on the lower right. OSKAR FISCHEL, *Raffaels Zeichnungen*, Berlin 1913-1941, no. 373, pp. 383f.; ECKHART KNAB, ERWIN MITSCH and KONRAD OBERHUBER, with SYLVIA FERINO-PAGDEN, *Raphael: Die Zeichnungen*, Stuttgart 1983, no. 425; PAUL JOANNIDES, op. cit. (note 22), no. 325. – The other one in the Berlin Kupferstichkabinett (inv. no. 2231) already has the young Saint John. FISCHEL, ibid., no. 374; KNAB, MITSCH and OBERHUBER, ibid., no. 426; JOANNIDES, ibid., no. 326.

29 Summary in MEYER ZUR CAPELLEN, op. cit. (note 11), vol. 2: *The Roman Religious Paintings*, Landshut 2005, no. 58, pp. 144-149.

30 Summary by ALLEGRI in GREGORI 1984, op. cit (note 5), p. 168;

The *Madonna dell'Impannata* dates from Raphael's advanced Roman period, when the artist after his early concentration on the painterly execution of the *Stanza della Segnatura* once more began to paint devotional pictures and altarpieces. It seems that during these years Raphael painted not just for the Pope. We have some evidence that high clergymen also made efforts to obtain works by the artist. A passage in a missive from Beltrame Costabili to

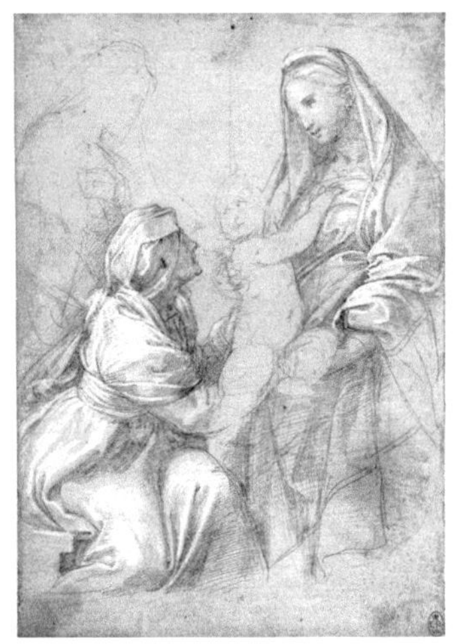

16 Study for the *Madonna dell'Impannata*, Windsor Castle.

Alfonso d'Este in Ferrara dated 4 December 1517 describes what probably was a characteristic situation in the time of Leo X. pontificate: '... *il Papa e questi Signori cardinali palatini li danno da fare assai.* ...'[31] The desire of the clergy probably referred less to portraits, as was the case with Pietro Bembo,[32] but rather to works with religious themes. It is generally assumed that Raphael's workshop increased in size during his advanced Roman years, but I believe this development was not only due to the manifold assignments Leo X. ordered the artist to execute. The vast number of early repeats of well-known compositions by Raphael suggests that these included also replicas which at the time left the workshop as "Raphaels" to satisfy the clergy's demands. This is a question that has barely been addressed in the relevant literature.

---

see also ALAN CHONG , op. cit. (note 27), pp. 380ff.

31 See SHEARMAN 2003, op. cit. (note 24), vol. 1, p. 311.

32 Thus Pietro Bembo remarks in a letter of 19 April 1516 to Cardinal Bibbiena '... *penso di farmi ritrarre ancho io un giorno.* ...' See SHEARMAN 2003, op. cit. (note 24), vol. 1, pp. 240ff. One may assume that many portraits of clergymen were included in the wall paintings of the *Stanza della Segnatura* who have not yet been identified.

When we discuss painted repetitions we have to distinguish clearly between copies and replicas. Copies are usually produced independently from the artist and his workshop and mainly at a later date. Replicas on the other hand are intimately connected with the artist's workshop: the artist himself may have re-

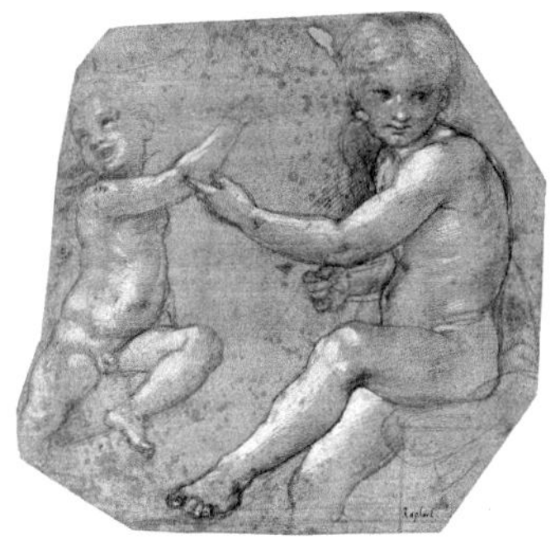

17 Study for the *Madonna dell'Impannata*, Berlin, Kupferstichkabinett.

peated his own work or left it to assistants. This leaves open the question whether and to what degree the artist supervised or personally intervened in the painterly execution. For a replica preparatory drawings for the first version could be used or else a cartoon. Where a replica differs markedly from important elements of the original work, it is identified as the first, second, etc. version.

Since we lack specific information about the working arrangements in Raphael's workshop, and both its structure and its site (presumably in the Vatican) are not mentioned in the documents,[33] we have to take a different path to obtain clarity about the practices in the workshop. Only a precise examination of early replicas can answer the question whether there are among the copies known today also replicas from Raphael's workshop. Should this be the case, each specimen needs to be assessed and every relevant work undergo a thorough technical examination. Only if we collect a large number of examined paintings it will be possible to arrive at a differentiated view of the developing practice in Raphael's workshop during his Roman period. For this the same criteria should be applied which were used for the specification of the painterly substance of an original work. This means that a technological analysis would at first examine

---

33 There are numerous, mainly short publications dealing with the workshop. We refer here only to the latest contribution by Pier Luigi de Vecchi, *Raffael*, Munich 2002, pp. 280ff., about the workshop's share of the late panel paintings pp. 305ff.

the support (wood or canvas) and compare its characteristics with the recorded data from the already examined original works. The next step would be an examination of the layers of paint, taking into account the condition and possibility of later changes. A prime consideration is the analysis of the pigments because painting materials in use only since the seventeenth century would rule out a dating to the sixteenth century. Finally X-ray and infra-red reflectography also make it possible to assess the genesis of a painting. Even if all the technical analyses proof positive, in the end it is the stylistic criticism and placing that counts: the work in question has to be connected convincingly with other proven and more or less authentic works by the artist and his workshop.

Many painted repetitions and repeated engravings are known of the *Madonna dell'Impanata*, an indication of its huge popularity and appreciation for far into the nineteenth century. The earliest print after the painting was made by Francesco Villamena in 1602 (fig. 18).[34] His annotation implies that the copy used was not the one held by the Galleria Palatina, but instead a version owned by Matteo di Capua Principe di Conca (d. 1607) and kept in Naples. In the city guide produced in 1607 by Giulio Cesare Capaccio he describes in the former's collection a highly treasured panel painting which undoubtedly showed a *Madonna dell'Impannata*.[35] The engraving of 1602, like

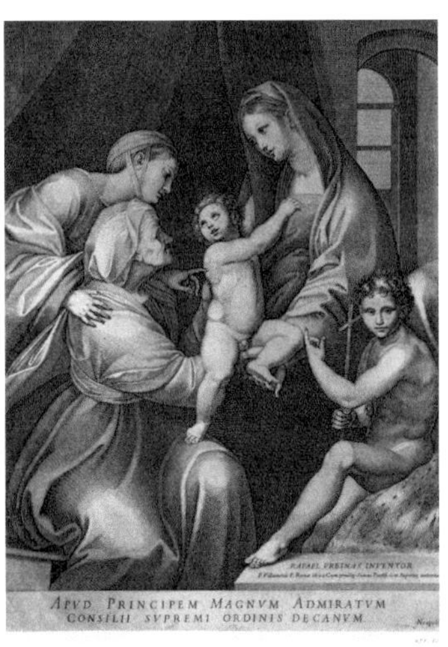

18 *Madonna dell'Impannata*, engraving, 1602, Berlin, Kupferstichkabinett.

---

34 Berlin, Kupferstichkabinett, inv. no. 421-1898; sheet size: 43,5 x 30,0 cm; height x width of the engraving 40,6 x 29,7 cm.

35 Capaccio's text reads: *'Raphelis Urbinatis tabula in qua B. Virgo, filius, Iohannes Baptista, D. Anna, in quibus nihil desiderare*

the *Madonna dell'Impannata Northwick*, does not show the lattice-like pattern of the *panni* on the back window, which raises the question whether the engraving was directly copied from the painting.[36]

---

spectator queat.' The annotation by Villamena reads: 'RAFAEL VRBINAS INVENTOR / *F. Villamena F. Romae 1602 Cum priuilegi Summi Pontificis et Superior authoritate.* / APVD PRINCIPEM MAGNVM ADMIRATVM CONSILII SVPREMI ORDINIS DECANVM.' For details see GRAZIA BERNINI PEZZINI et al., *Raphael invenit: Stampe da Raffaello nelle collezioni dell'Istituto nazionale per la grafica,* Rome 1985, pp. 201f.

36 See, for instance, the engraving of 1825 by Esquivel de Sotomayor made in Florence. – The multitude of prints as well as painted repetitions of the *Madonna dell'Impanata* dates not earlier than the nineteenth century. See ETTORE ALLEGRI in GREGORI 1984, op. cit. (note 5), pp. 170f.; see too RAINER MICHAEL MASON and NATALE MAURO, *Raphael et la seconde main,* Geneva 1984, pp. 231ff., and CORINNA HÖPER et al., *Raffael und die Folgen: Das Kunstwerk im Zeitalter seiner graphischen Reproduzierbarkeit,* Stuttgart 2001, pp. 304f. – A meticulous examination of this material may produce interesting insights into Raphael's workshop's practices.

IV. Plates

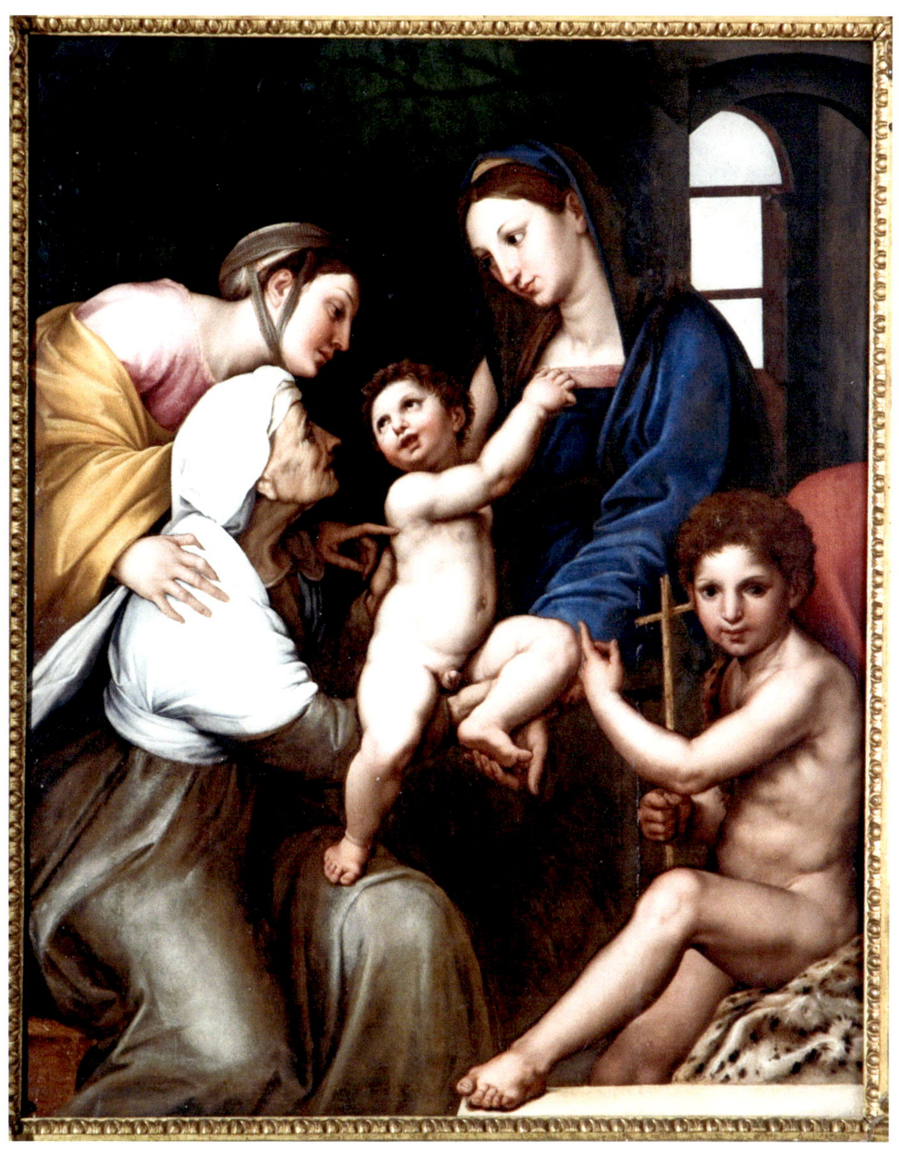

I   *Madonna dell'Impannata Northwick*,
oil on poplar,
150,8 x 121,3 cm,
private collection.

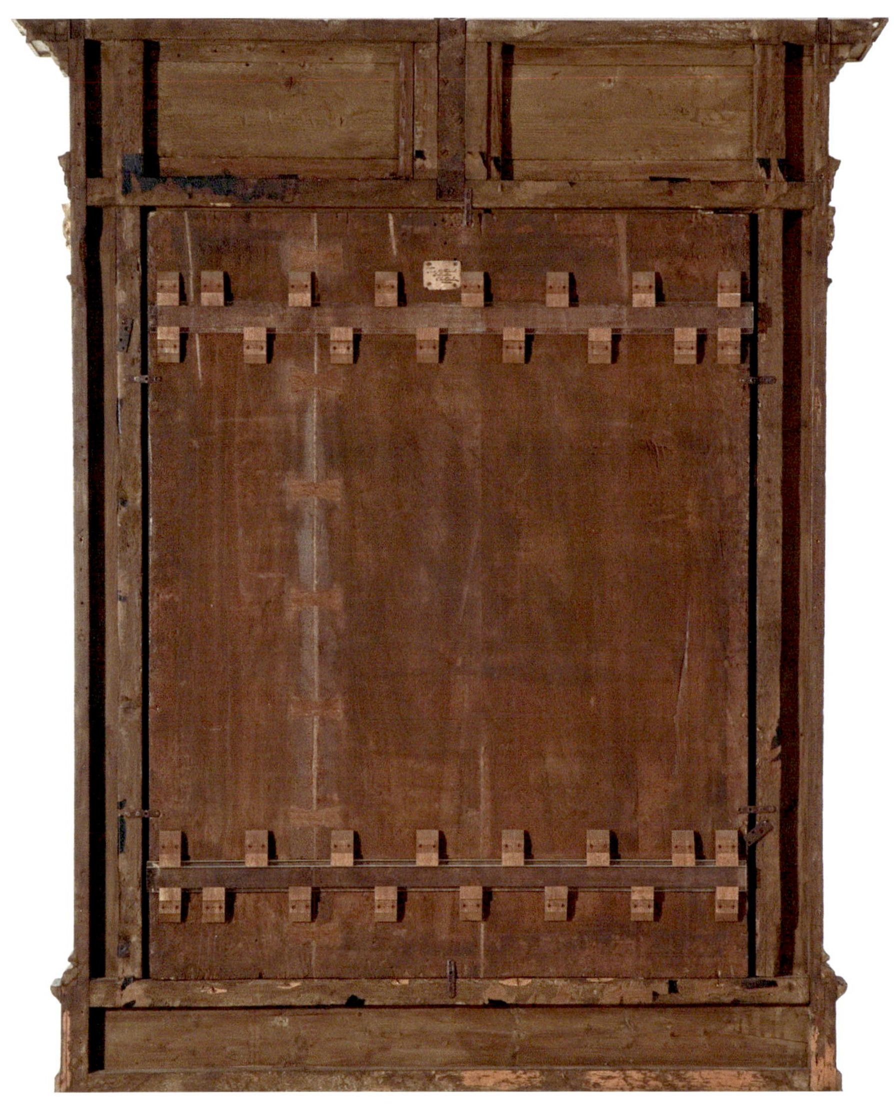

II   *Madonna dell'Impannata Northwick,*
     back of the framed painting.

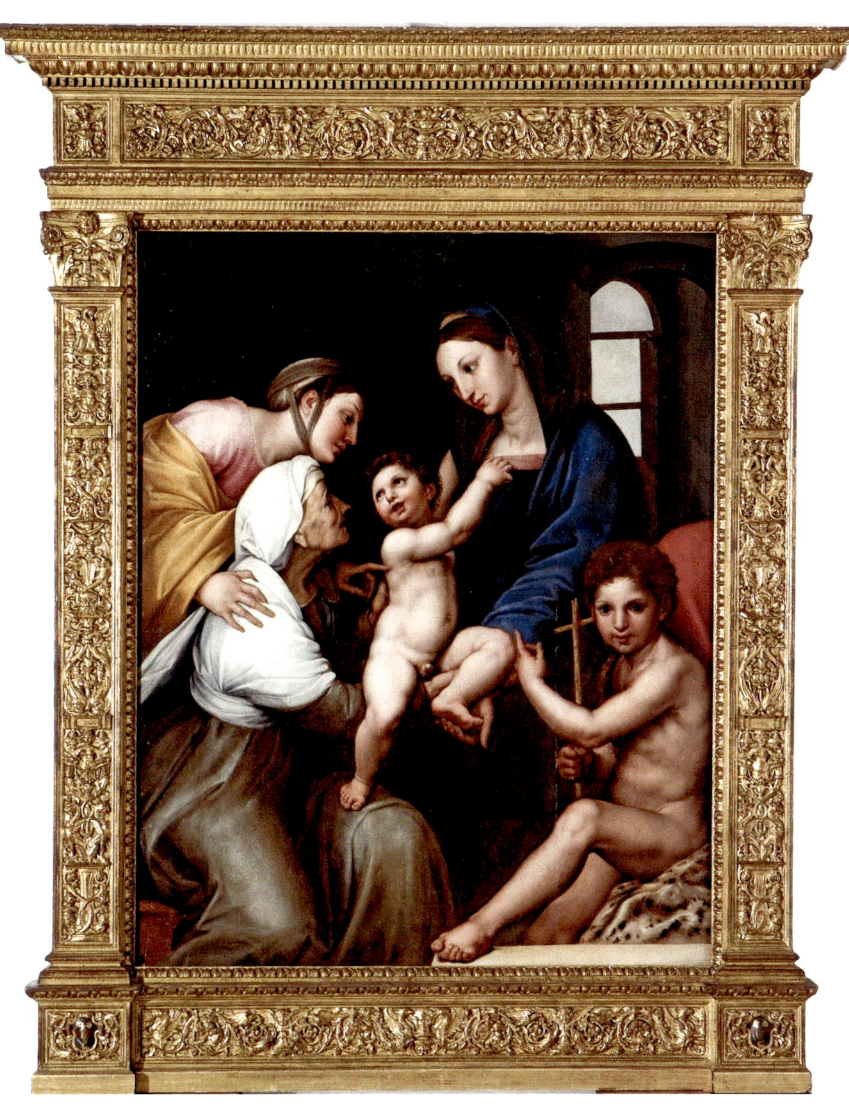

III   *Madonna dell'Impannata Northwick,*
in frame.

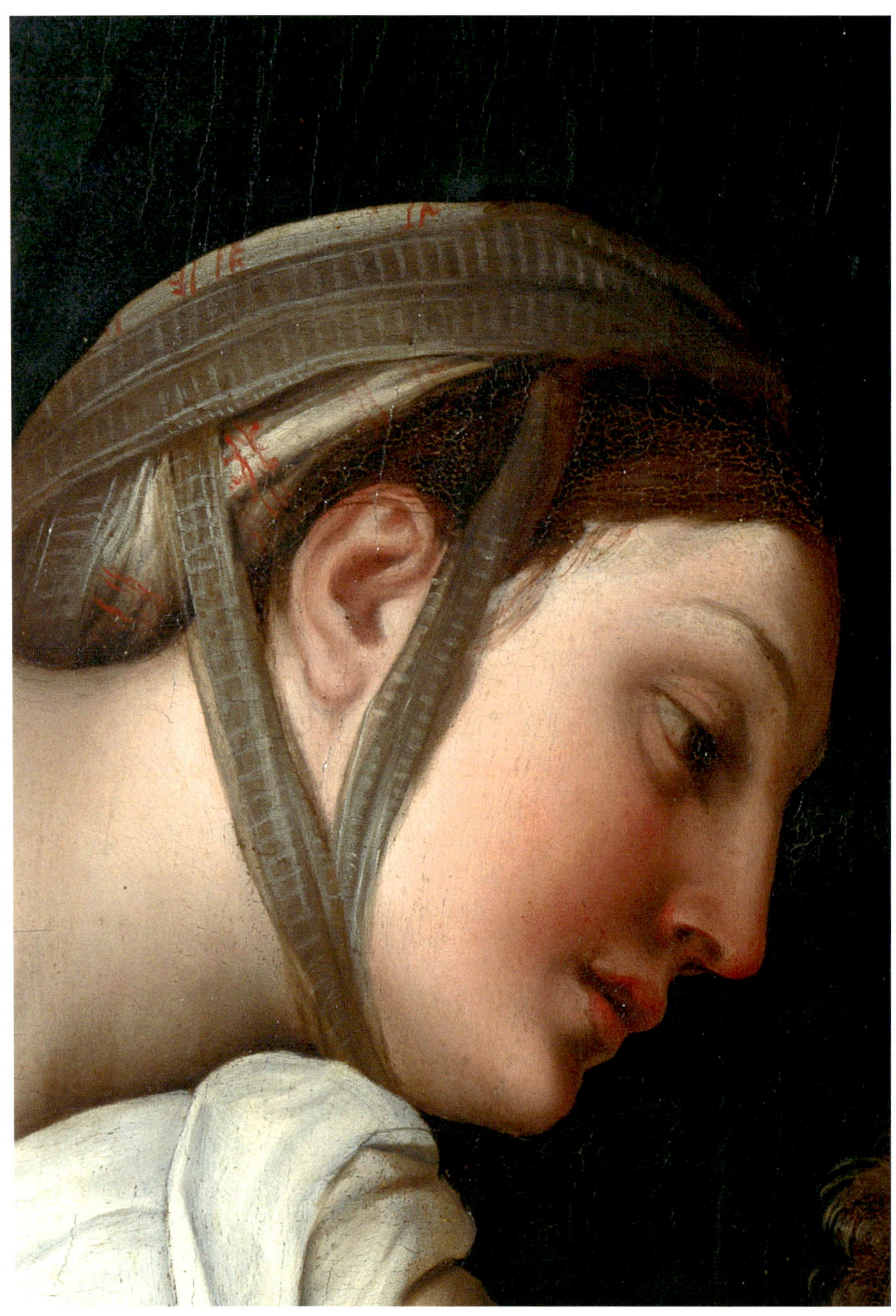

IV *Madonna dell'Impannata Northwick*,
detail of the head of a female Saint.

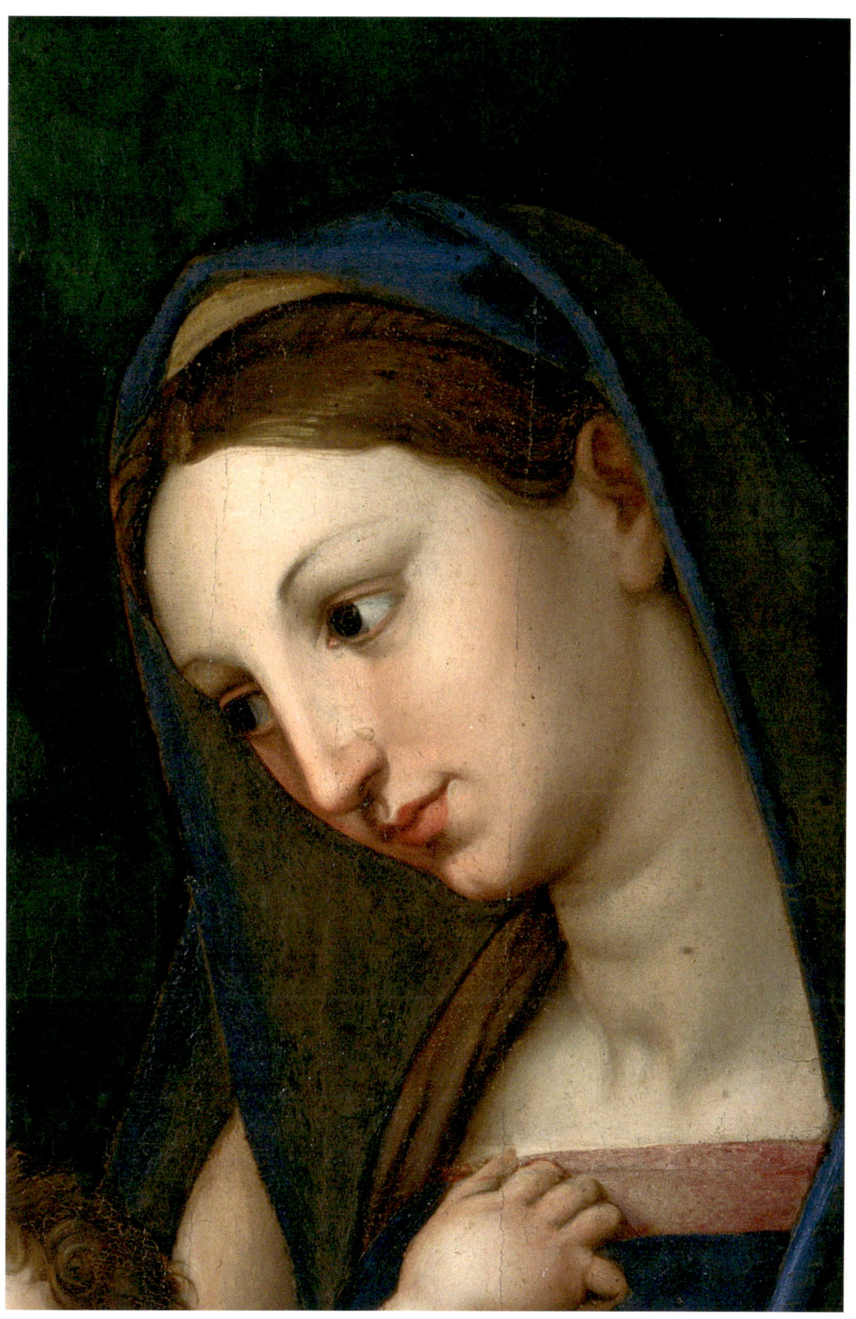

V *Madonna dell'Impannata Northwick,*
detail of the head of the Virgin.

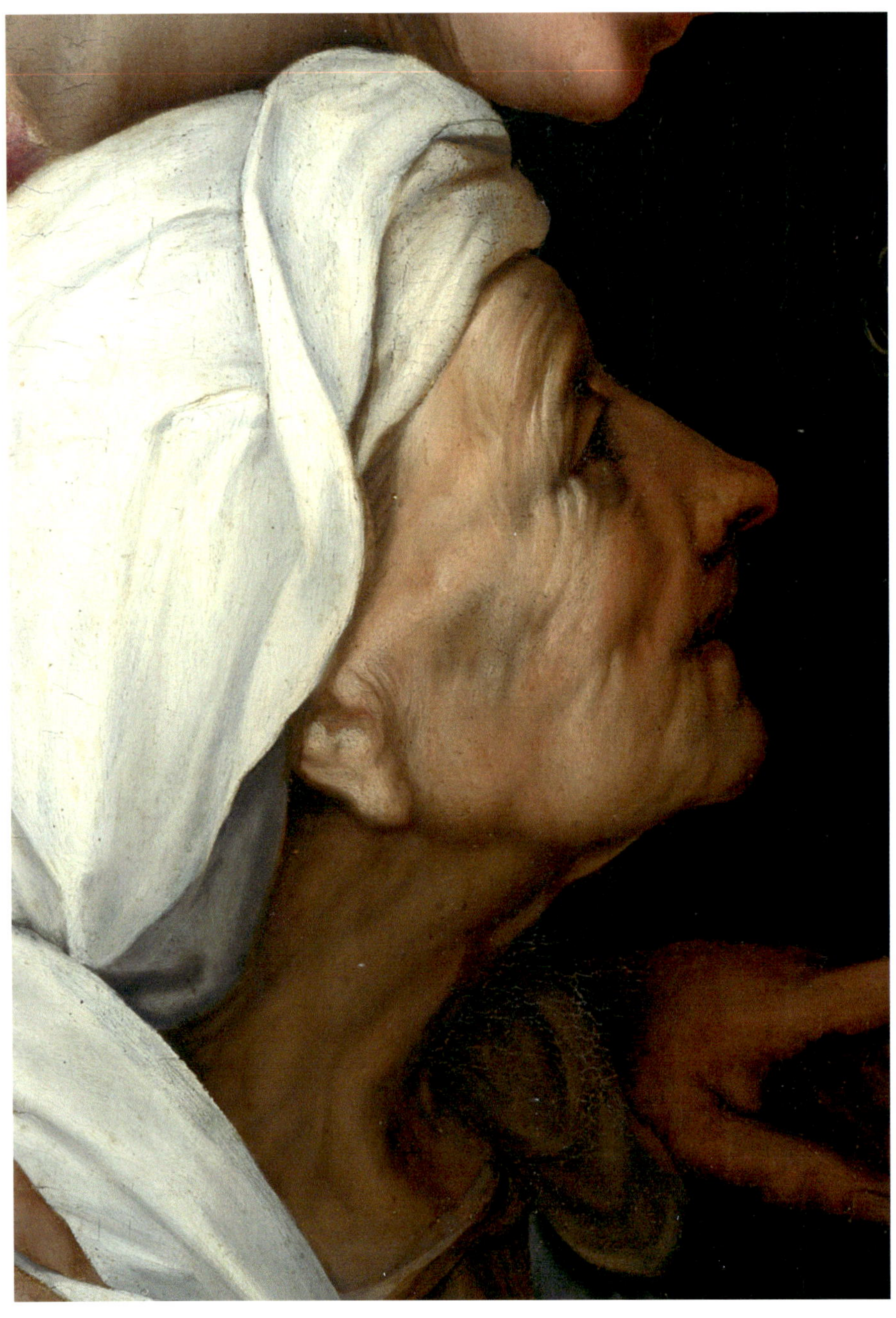

VI *Madonna dell'Impannata Northwick,*
detail of the head of Saint Anna.

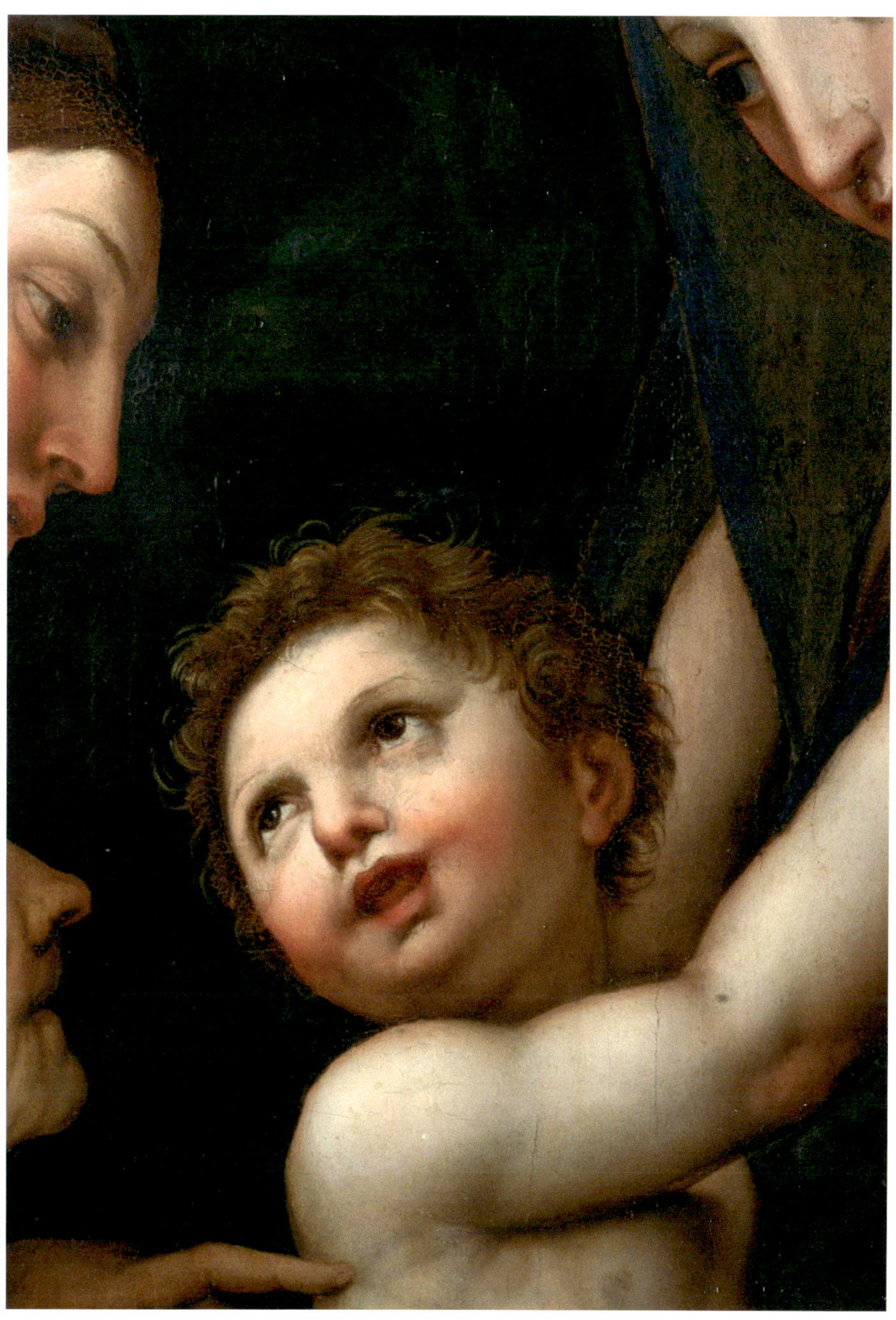

VII   *Madonna dell'Impannata Northwick*,
detail of the head of Christ Child.

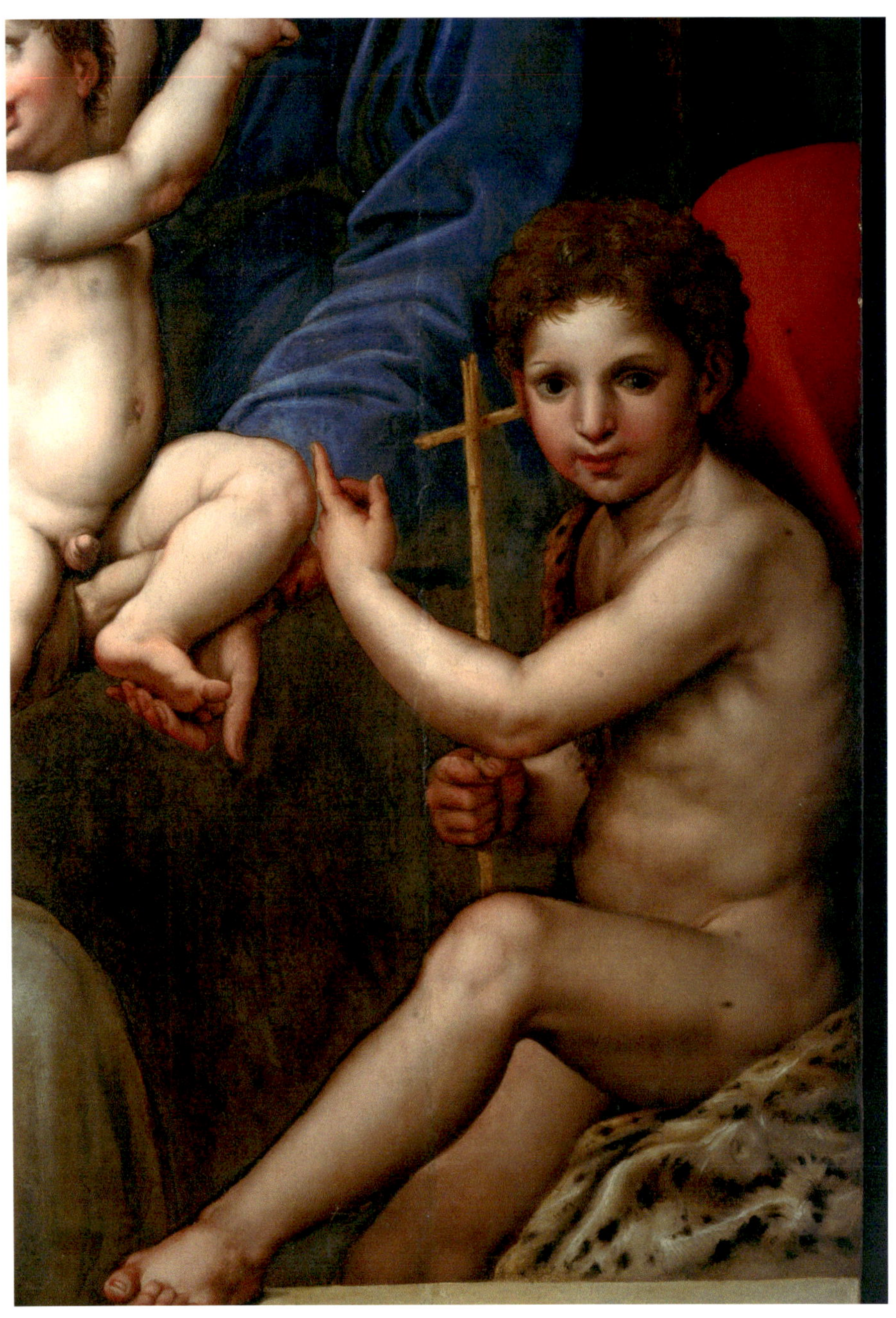

VIII   *Madonna dell'Impannata Northwick,*
detail of Saint John the Baptist.

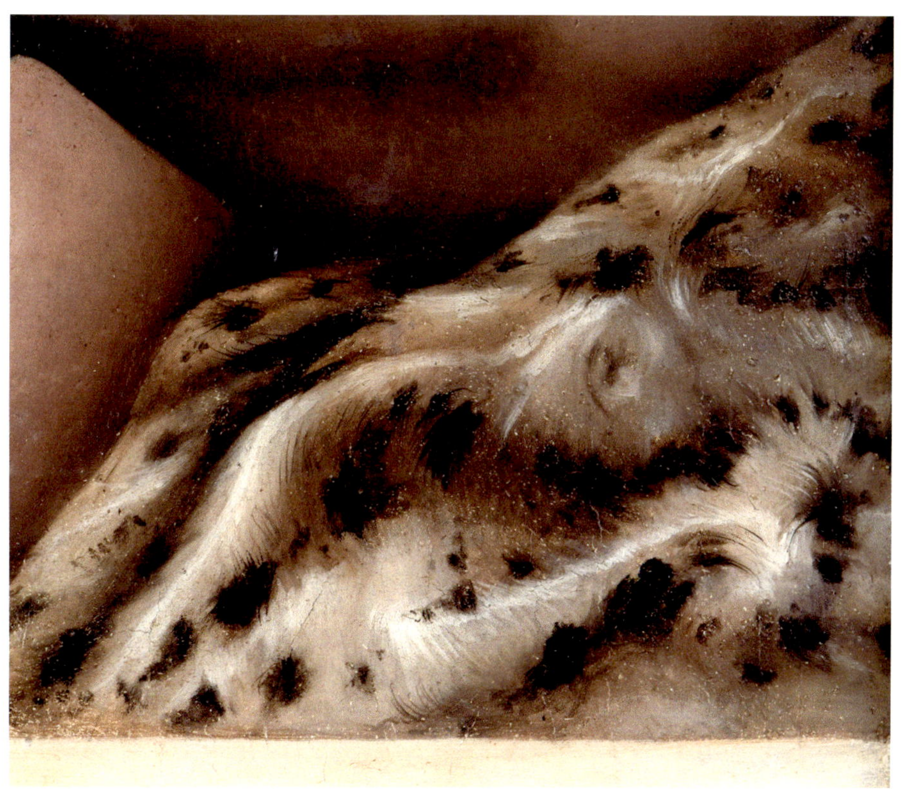

IX   *Madonna dell'Impannata Northwick*,
detail of the leopard's hide.

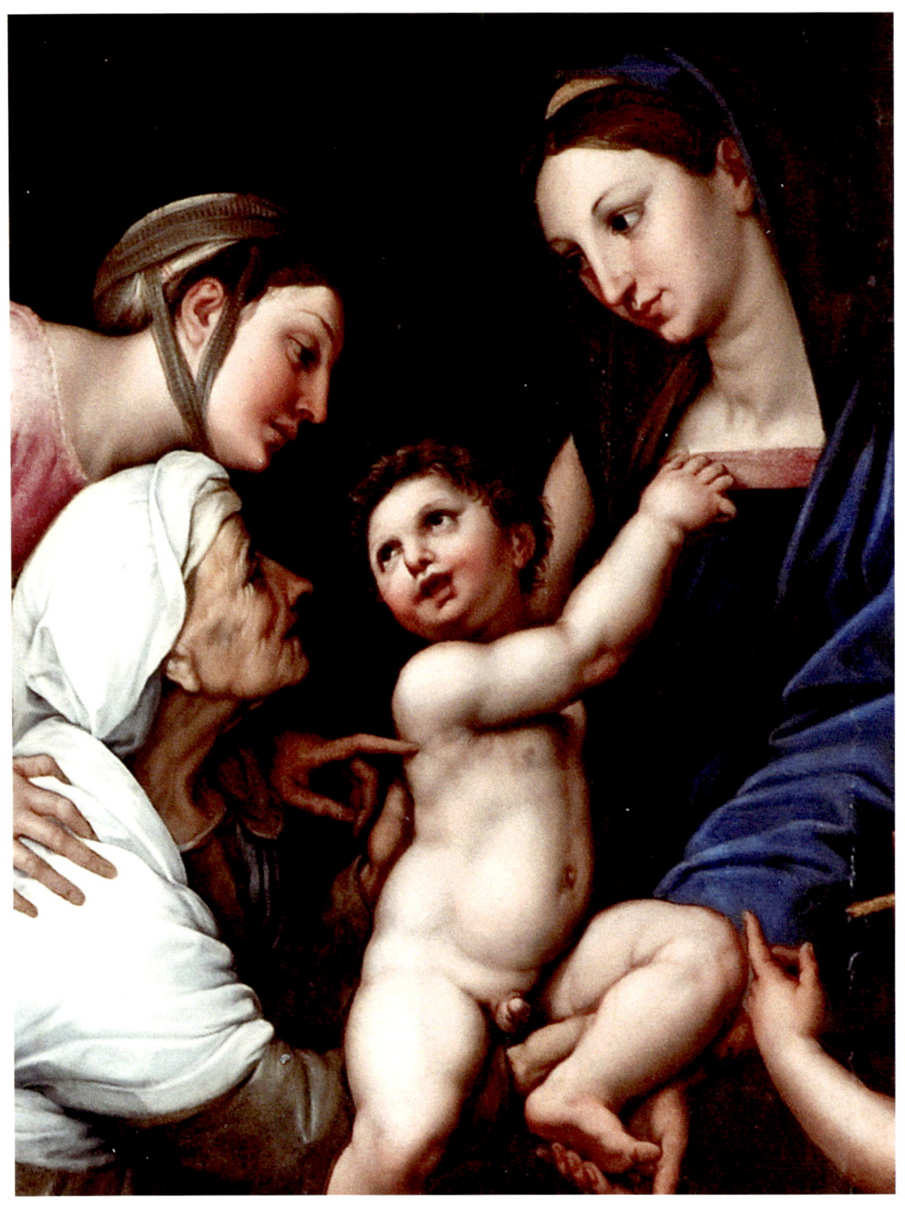

X *Madonna dell'Impannata Northwick,*
detail of the central group.

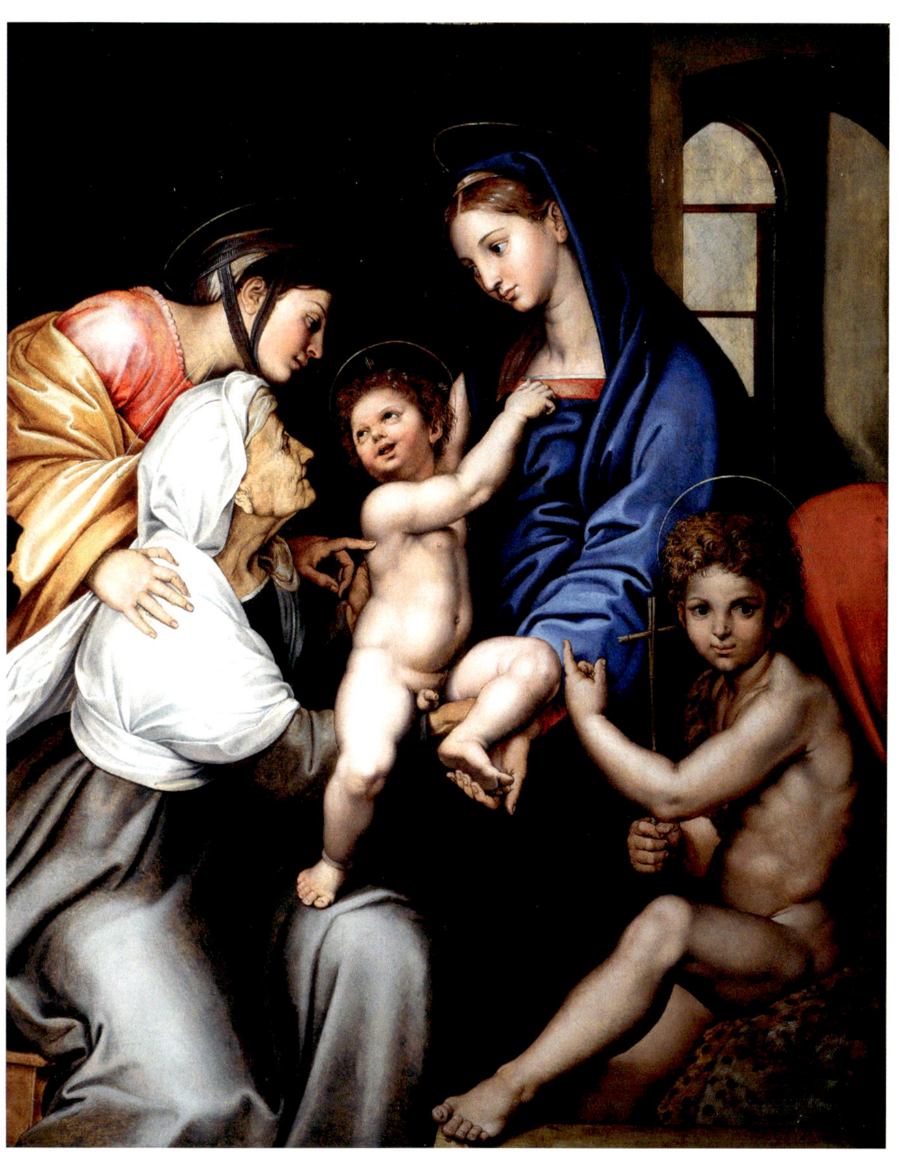

XI *Madonna dell'Impannata,*
panel,
152,39 x 122,55 cm,
Corsham Court.

V. APPENDIX 1

**Restauration Report from January 2008
by Nicola Restauri, Aramengo (Torino)**

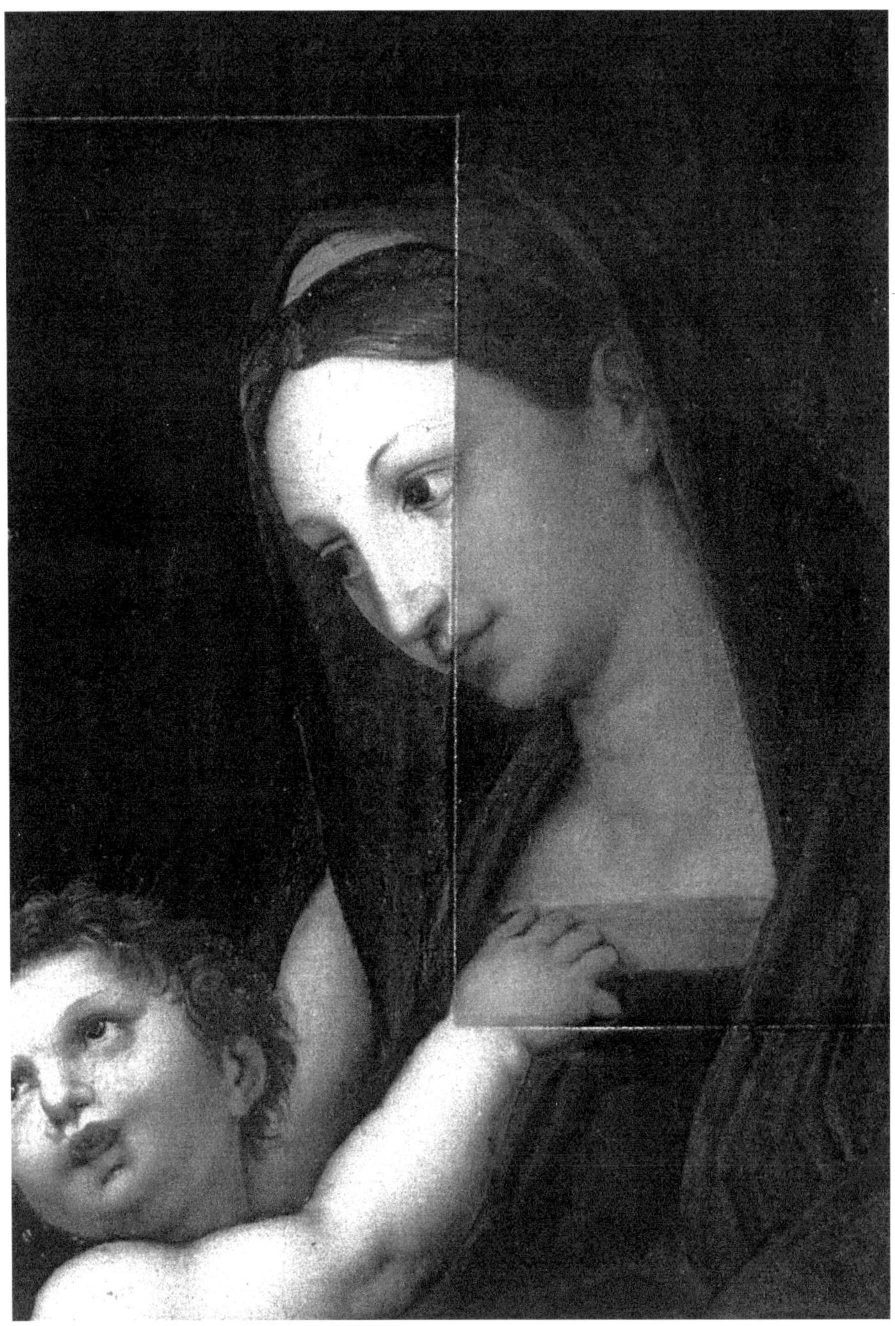

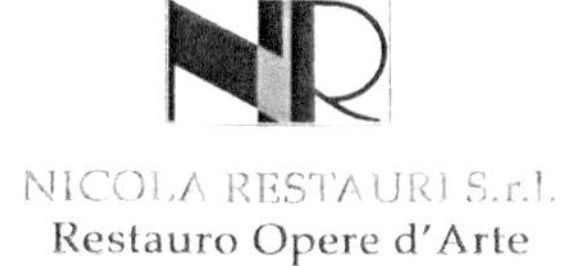

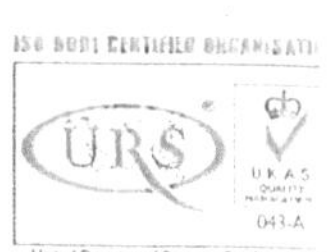

LABORATORIO
14020 ARAMENGO (AT), Via Mazzini, 8
tel. +39.0141.909125-26
fax +39.0141.909170
www.nicolarestauri.com
e-mail: info@nicolarestauri.com

SEDE AMMINISTRATIVA E LEGALE
10124 TORINO - Via Santa Giulia, 65
tel e fax +39.011.8122780

NICOLA RESTAURI S.r.l.
Restauro Opere d'Arte

Studio e progettazione interventi di restauro
Analisi, Esami all'U.V., RX, Riflettografie in I.R.

Raffaello (attr.) *Madonna dell'Impannata*
dipinto su tavola cm 160 x 100
150,8 x 121,3

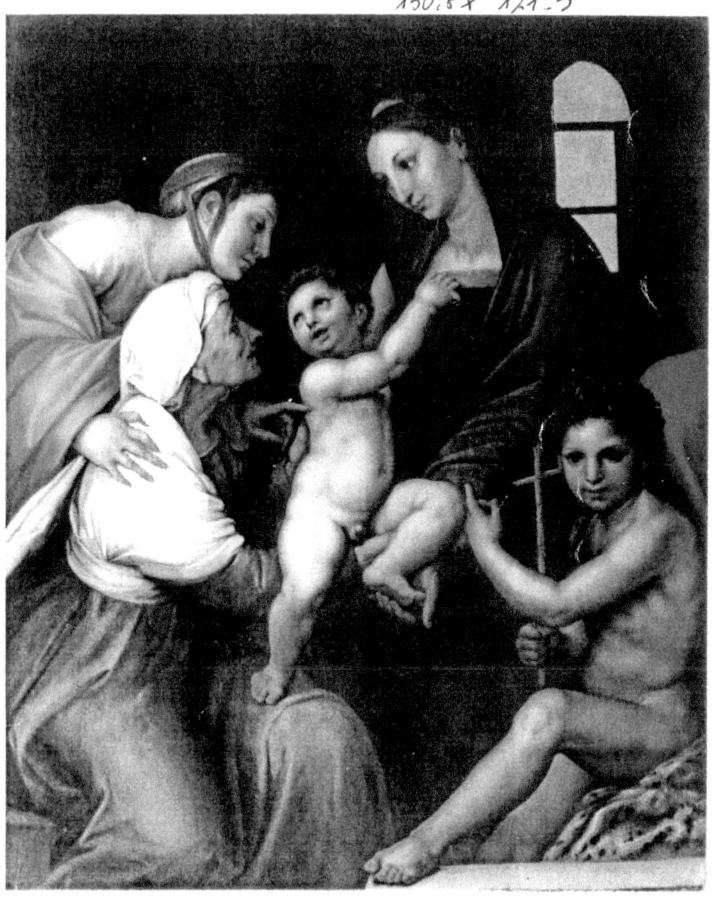

Cod. Fisc. e Partita IVA 05422100015 - Capitale Sociale €12.000,00 Int.Vers. - C.C.I.A.A. Torino N.711779 - Trib di Torino N.240/88 Reg.Soc

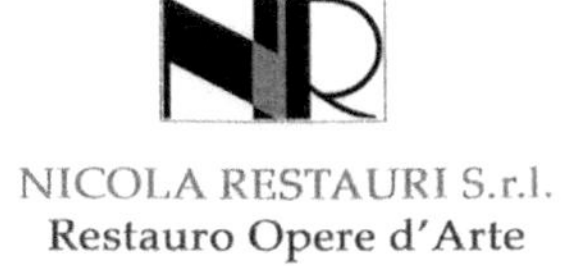

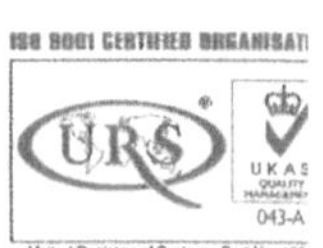

LABORATORIO
14020 ARAMENGO (AT), Via Mazzini, 8
tel. +39.0141909125-26
fax +39.0141.909170
www.nicolarestauri.com
e-mail: info@nicolarestauri.com

SEDE AMMINISTRATIVA E LEGALE
10124 TORINO - Via Santa Giulia, 65
tel e fax. +39.011.8122780

NICOLA RESTAURI S.r.l.
Restauro Opere d'Arte

Studio e progettazione interventi di restauro
Analisi, Esami all'U.V., RX, Riflettografie in I.R.

Il dipinto era stato sottoposto a restauro presso il nostro laboratorio nel 1992. In quella occasione era stato osservato all'UV, con Riflettografia ed era stata realizzata una lastra radiografica a campione.

Come richiesto, la tavola è stata oggi sottoposta ad una indagine radiografica completa sull'intera superficie dipinta, al fine di evidenziare le condizioni conservative, la tecnica esecutiva ed eventuali anomalie.

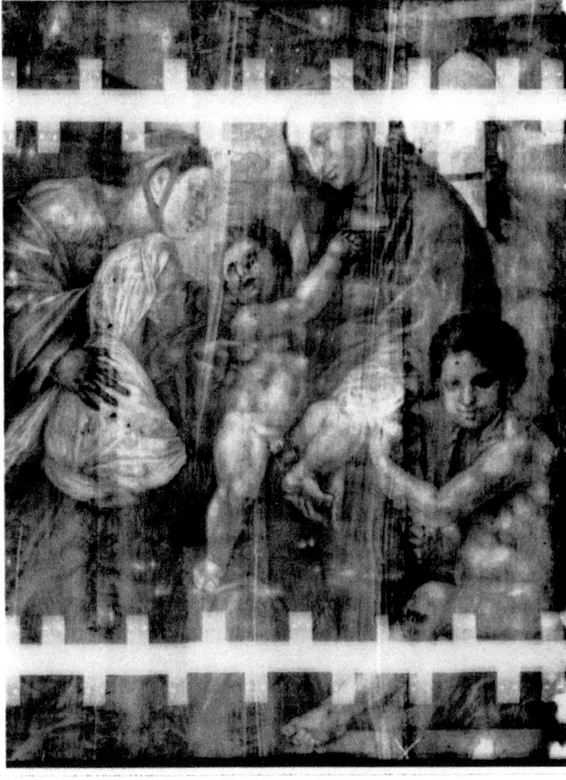

Sono state realizzate 18 esposizioni radiografiche digitali successivamente assemblate a computer. E' stata impiegata una innovativa tecnica digitale ad alta definizione (sistema DURR HD-CR 35 NDT) che utilizza cristalli di fosforo al posto dei tradizionali cristalli d'argento.

L'indagine rileva uno stato di conservazione quasi ottimale; le perdite di colore sono ridotte sia nel numero che nell'estensione ed anche le abrasioni non sono significative. La materia pittorica è

Cod. Fisc. e Partita IVA 05422100015 - Capitale Sociale €12.000,00 Int.Vers. - C.C.I.A.A. Torino N.711779 - Trib di Torino N.240/88 Reg.Soc

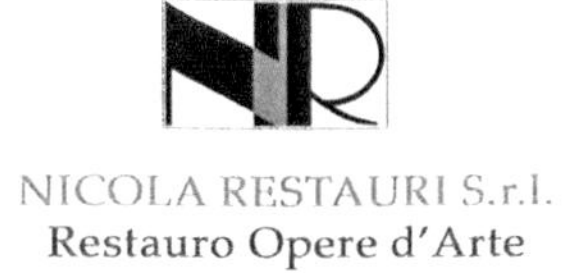

NICOLA RESTAURI S.r.l.
Restauro Opere d'Arte

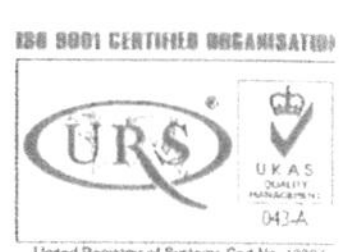

LABORATORIO
14020 ARAMENGO (AT), Via Mazzini, 8
tel. +39.0141909125-26
fax +39.0141.909170
www.nicolarestauri.com
e-mail: info@nicolarestauri.com

SEDE AMMINISTRATIVA E LEGALE
10124 TORINO - Via Santa Giulia, 65
tel e fax. +39.011.8122780

Studio e progettazione interventi di restauro
Analisi, Esami all'U.V., RX, Riflettografie in I.R.

compatta e corposa, in alcune zone con pennellate dense stese a spessore. La radiografia rivela un abbondante utilizzo di biacca (bianco di piombo) per il cielo, gli incarnati e naturalmente per il velo bianco sul capo di S. Elisabetta. Ai Raggi X emerge con chiarezza sul lato superiore e sul lato destro la sagoma di un albero o di un ramo con molte foglie che già si intravede ad occhio nudo illuminando il dipinto con una buona luce. E' più probabile che si tratti di un pentimento piuttosto che del riutilizzo del supporto, già parzialmente dipinto.

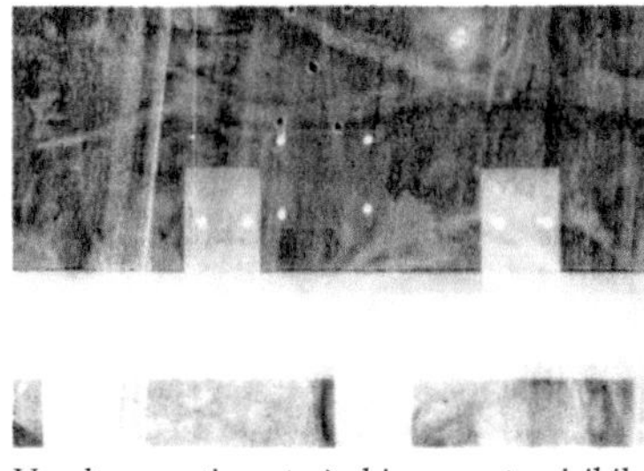
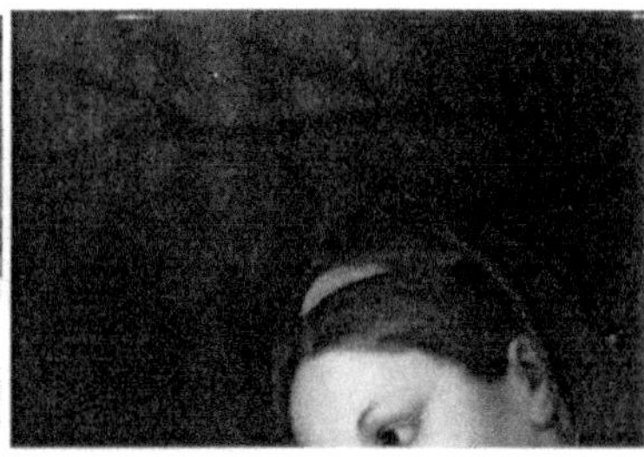

Un altro pentimento è chiaramente visibile ai raggi X anche in corrispondenza del volto di S. Elisabetta (mento e naso).

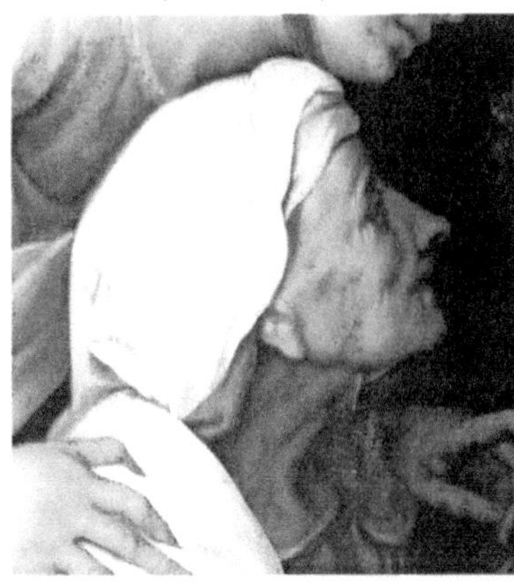
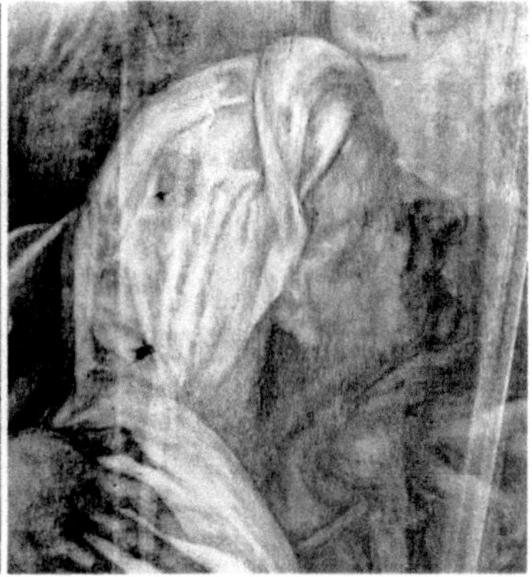

Cod. Fisc. e Partita IVA 05422100015 - Capitale Sociale €12.000,00 Int.Vers. - C.C.I.A.A. Torino N.711779 - Trib di Torino N.240/88 Reg.Soc

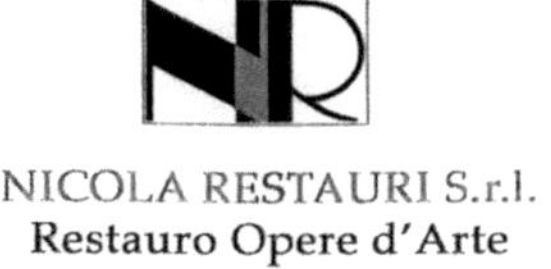
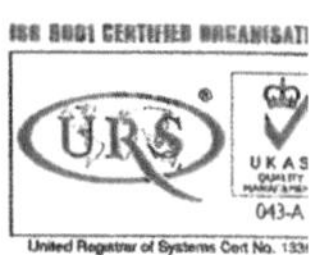

LABORATORIO
14020 ARAMENGO (AT), Via Mazzini, 8
tel. +39.0141909125-26
fax +39.0141.909170
www.nicolarestauri.com
e-mail: info@nicolarestauri.com

SEDE AMMINISTRATIVA E LEGALE
10124 TORINO - Via Santa Giulia, 65
tel e fax. +39.011.8122780

NICOLA RESTAURI S.r.l.
Restauro Opere d'Arte

Studio e progettazione interventi di restauro
Analisi, Esami all'U.V., RX, Riflettografie in I.R.

L'opera è stata inoltre esaminata all'Infrarosso; è stato realizzato un particolare del volto di Gesù Bambino con fotocamera digitale alla profondità di 1100 nm. L'esame ha messo in evidenza solo alcuni tratti del disegno preparatorio, la pellicola pittorica è infatti, come si è detto, piuttosto spessa. E' stata quindi realizzata, sull'intera superficie e registrata in 12 particolari, la Riflettografia in I.R. (con apparecchiatura HAMAMATSU, videocamera C 2400-03 d, tubo VIDICON + filtro addizionale I.R. e risposta spettrale fino a 2400 nm).

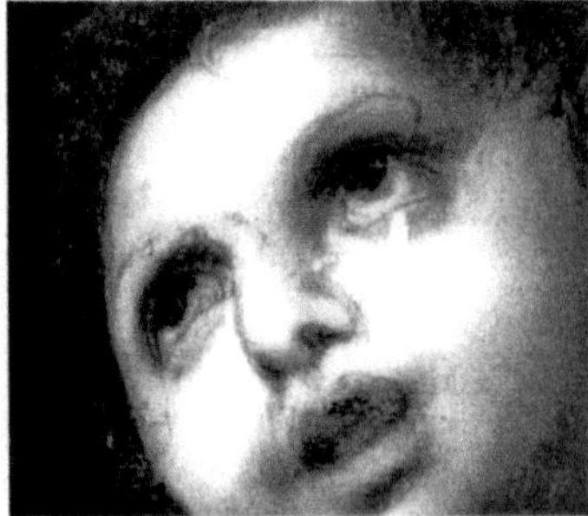
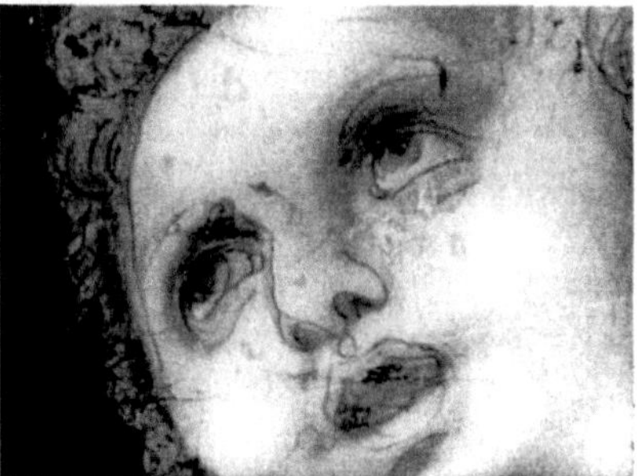

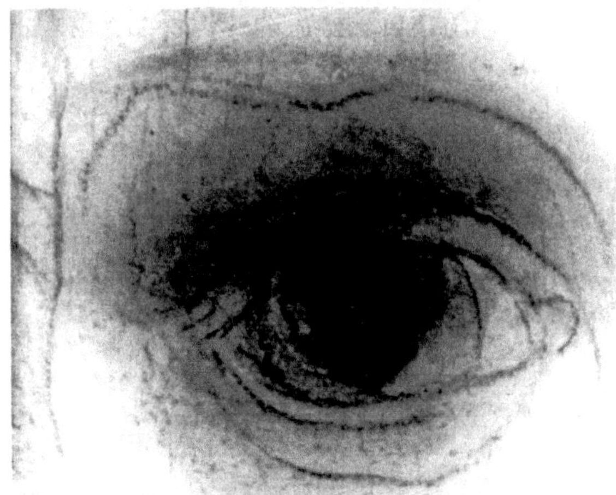

L'indagine ha rivelato molto chiaramente che il disegno è realizzato a carboncino con tratti netti limitati ai contorni. Non sono state ritrovate tracce di spolvero, tuttavia è possibile che il disegno, in alcune zone come

Cod. Fisc. e Partita IVA 05422100015 - Capitale Sociale €12.000,00 Int.Vers. - C.C.I.A.A. Torino N.711779 - Trib di Torino N.240/88 Reg.Soc

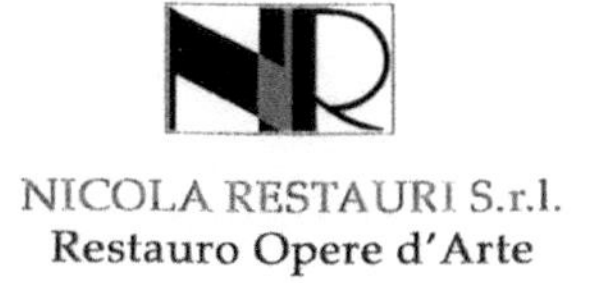

NICOLA RESTAURI S.r.l.
Restauro Opere d'Arte

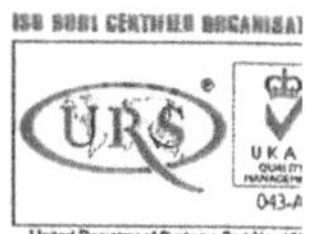

LABORATORIO
14020 ARAMENGO (AT), Via Mazzini, 8
tel. +39.0141909125-26
fax +39.0141.909170
www.nicolarestauri.com
e-mail: info@nicolarestauri.com

SEDE AMMINISTRATIVA E LEGALE
10124 TORINO · Via Santa Giulia, 65
tel e fax. +39.011.8122780

Studio e progettazione interventi di restauro
Analisi, Esami all'U.V., RX, Riflettografie in I.R.

sul volto del Gesù Bambino, più rigido se paragonato a quello rilevato su certe altre opere dell'Artista[1], sia riportato da cartone. Sono stati rilevati pentimenti in corrispondenza degli occhi, dell'orecchio e delle mani della santa a sinistra, della bocca e della mano destra di San Giovannino e ancora in corrispondenza del naso di S. Elisabetta.

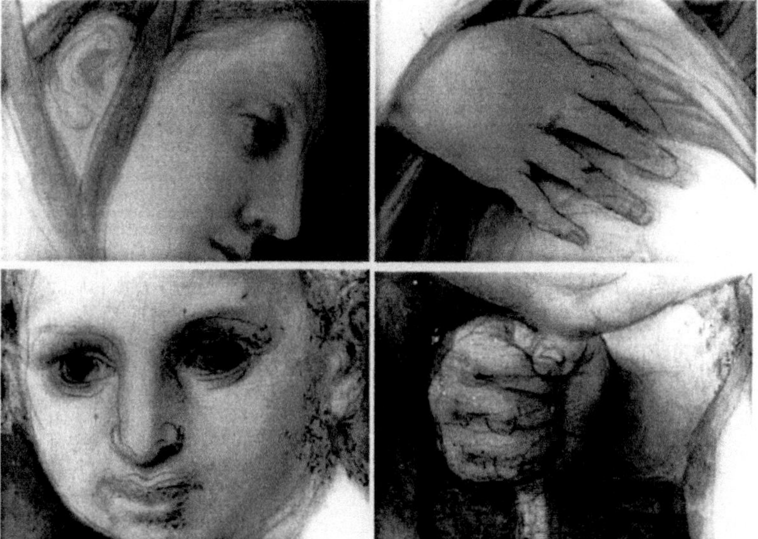

L'ampia documentazione fotografica delle analisi eseguite, trasmessa in allegato, potrà fornire agli studiosi, storici e critici d'arte, elementi utili per l'approfondimento attributivo.

Direttore Tecnico Responsabile
Anna Rosa Nicola

NICOLA RESTAURI S.r.l
Nicola Pisano

---

[1] Raphael's painting technique: working practices before Rome- Proceedings of the Eu-ARTECH workshop - Edited by Ashok Roy and Marika Spring - Kermes quaderni- Nardini Editore Firenze 2007

Cod. Fisc. e Partita IVA 05422100015 - Capitale Sociale €12.000,00 Int.Vers. - C.C.I.A.A. Torino N.711779 - Trib di Torino N.240/88 Reg.Soc

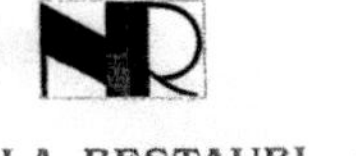

Sede amministrativa e legale:
10124 TORINO - Via Santa Giulia, 65
tel. e fax +39.011.812.27.80

Laboratorio:
14020 ARAMENGO (AT) - Via Mazzini, 8
tel. +39.0141.90.91.25÷26
fax +39.0141.90.91.70
http: www.nicolarestauri.it
e-mail: nicolarestauri@tin.it

NICOLA RESTAURI s.r.l.
Restauro Opere d'Arte

Studio e progettazione interventi di restauro
Analisi, esami all'U.V., RX - Riflettografie in I.R.

"Madonna dell'Impannata"

Opera cinqucentesca, dipinto ad olio su tavola, cm 150.8x121.3

RELAZIONE DI RESTAURO

Lo stato di conservazione della tavola, al momento del suo arrivo nei nostri laboratori, presentava alcune problematiche legate all'effetto delle variazioni termoigrometriche sul supporto ligneo, all'azione degli xilofagi e all'alterazioni dei precedenti interventi di restauro sulla pellicola pittorica.

Il retro della tavola denunciava in particolare numerose fenditure e rotture che forzando i naturali micromovimenti delle fibre lignee, provocavano sul lato dipinto difetti di adesione tra gli strati (legno/preparazione/colore) con conseguente formazione di craquelure e sollevamento di alcune scaglie; le vecchie cadute di pellicola erano state in precedenza pittoricamente risarcite e mostravano ormai alterazioni del tono.

I diffusi fori di sfarfallamento del tarlo e le profonde gallerie avevano inoltre provocato un generale indebolimento della consistenza materica, con la conseguente perdita di una piccola porzione nell'angolo inferiore sinistro (guardando la tavola da retro).

Si notavano alcuni frammenti di carta colorata di recupero incollati sul retro della tavola, Osservando il lato dipinto si notava un generale offuscamento dei toni originali, sia per la patina di depositi superficiali di polvere, smog ed altre sostanze estranee, sia per l'ossidazione dei protettivi a vernice stesi in passato; dal bordo inferiore, nella porzione

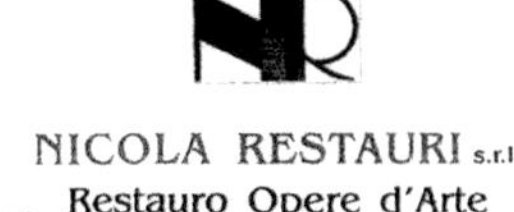

Sede amministrativa e legale:
10124 TORINO - Via Santa Giulia, 65
tel. e fax +39.011.812.27.80

Laboratorio:
14020 ARAMENGO (AT) - Via Mazzini, 8
tel. +39.0141.90.91.25-26
fax +39.0141.90.91.70
http: www.nicolarestauri.it
e-mail: nicolarestauri@tin.it

NICOLA RESTAURI s.r.l.
Restauro Opere d'Arte

Studio e progettazione interventi di restauro
Analisi, esami all'U.V., RX - Riflettografie in I.R.

destra, correva verso l'alto un'evidente fenditura del legno, ripresa pittoricamente in tono nei precedenti interventi di restauro.

Prima di procedere al restauro sul lato dipinto si è reso necessario eseguire alcune operazioni di risanamento del supporto ligneo, provvedendo all'eliminazione dei frammenti di carta incollati sul retro e dei residui di adesivo; rimossi anche i depositi superficiali, si sono effettuati i necessari trattamenti consolidanti ed antitarlo del legno. In corrispondenza delle varie rotture e fenditure, in base all'esigenza, sono state realizzate incollature e/o innesti. La piccola porzione angolare inferiore (andata in passato perduta) è stata volumetricamente ripristinata.

Terminato il trattamento sul retro, si è verificata l'adesione del colore e della preparazione ed aperti alcuni tasselli a campione, al fine di individuare i solventi idonei per la pulitura. Con un'apposita miscela di tensioattivi sono stati rimossi i protettivi ingialliti ed asportata la patina consistente di depositi generici (polvere, smog..); le riprese ed i rifacimenti sono stati eliminati con solvente previamente testato.

La delaminazione delle stuccature è stata condotta a bisturi; si sono infine risarcite le mancanze con stuccature a livello e reintegrazione pittorica in tono.

La superficie dipinta è stata infine sottoposta a trattamento protettivo mediante nebulizzazione di un velo di vernice sintetica, non ingiallente.

Laboratorio Nicola

NICOLA RESTAURI S.r.l.

NICOLA RESTAURI srl
L'Amministratore Unico

VI. APPENDIX 2

**Technological Report from May 2010
by Claudio Falcucci (M.I.S.A.), Rome**

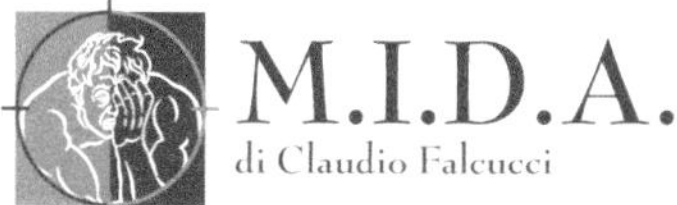

M.I.D.A.
di Claudio Falcucci

Metodologie d'Indagine per la Diagnostica Artistica

Madonna dell'Impannata (da)

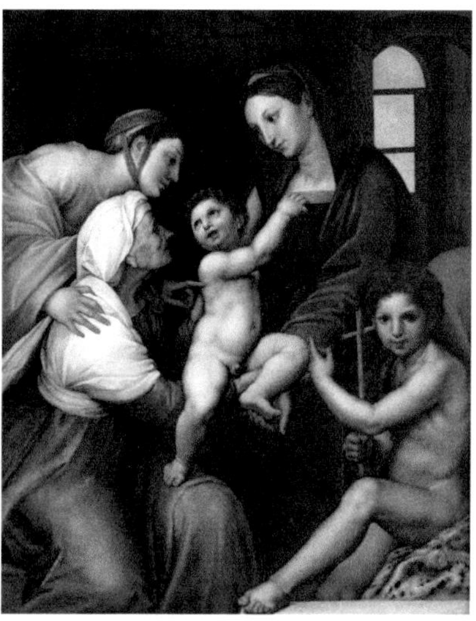

Indagini diagnostiche:
- Fluorescenza dei raggi X
- Riflettografia IR

M.I.D.A. di Claudio Falcucci
Via Leccosa, 15-16 - 00186 Roma - P. IVA 08704231003 - C.F. FLCCLD67E23C858T
Sede legale: via Aprilia, 12 - 00034 Colleferro (Roma)
tel. 06.68803992 - cell. 335.6768683
web-site: www.midaonline.com - e-mail: info@midaonline.com

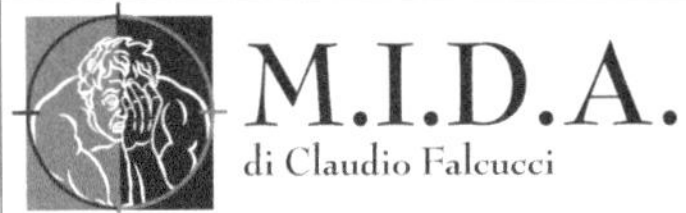

Notes

The painting was examined by means of X-ray fluorescence analyses and infrared reflectography, to characterize the pigments used by the author and to obtain some information about the underdrawing.

An underdrawing, not strictly respected by the painting layers, carries out the set up of the composition. The drawing seems to be transposed from a preliminar cardboard with the "ricalco" technique, to which can be attributed the small coal dots observed in the reflectographic detail from St.John's eye. The same image gives evidence of the differences between the drawing and the definitive image of the painting, where the eyes are slightly moved on the right side, while Child's eyes are slightly moved on the left. Some more changes between the drawing and the painting concerns, for example, the profiles of st. Anne and the right hand of St.John.

As regards the pigments, contrarily to the results obtained during previous analyses, the yellow robe is painted by using a lead-tin yellow pigment (giallorino) and yellow ochre, the red pillow close to st. John head is painted by using cinnabar while St.Elizabeth dress is obtained by using red lacquer.

Cinnabar, mixed to white lead and natural earths, is used also to paint the flesh tones.

A copper-based pigment, probably malachite, is used for the green tones from the trees, while the blue areas of Mary's cloak and St.Anne sleeves are painted by using smalt, a pigment obtained from a blue glass coloured with cobalt oxides and containing arsenic and nickel. This pigment spontaneously changed his colour becoming green or grey, while the persisting blue can be referred to the original ultramarine glaze applied on the blue smalt.

Roma, may 28th 2010

M.I.D.A. di Claudio Falcucci
Via Leccosa, 15/16 - 00186 Roma - P. IVA 08704231003 - C.F. FLCCLD67E23C858T
Sede legale: via Aprilia, 12 - 00034 Colleferro (Roma)
tel. 06.68803992 - cell. 335.6768683
web-site: www.midaonline.com   e-mail: info@midaonline.com

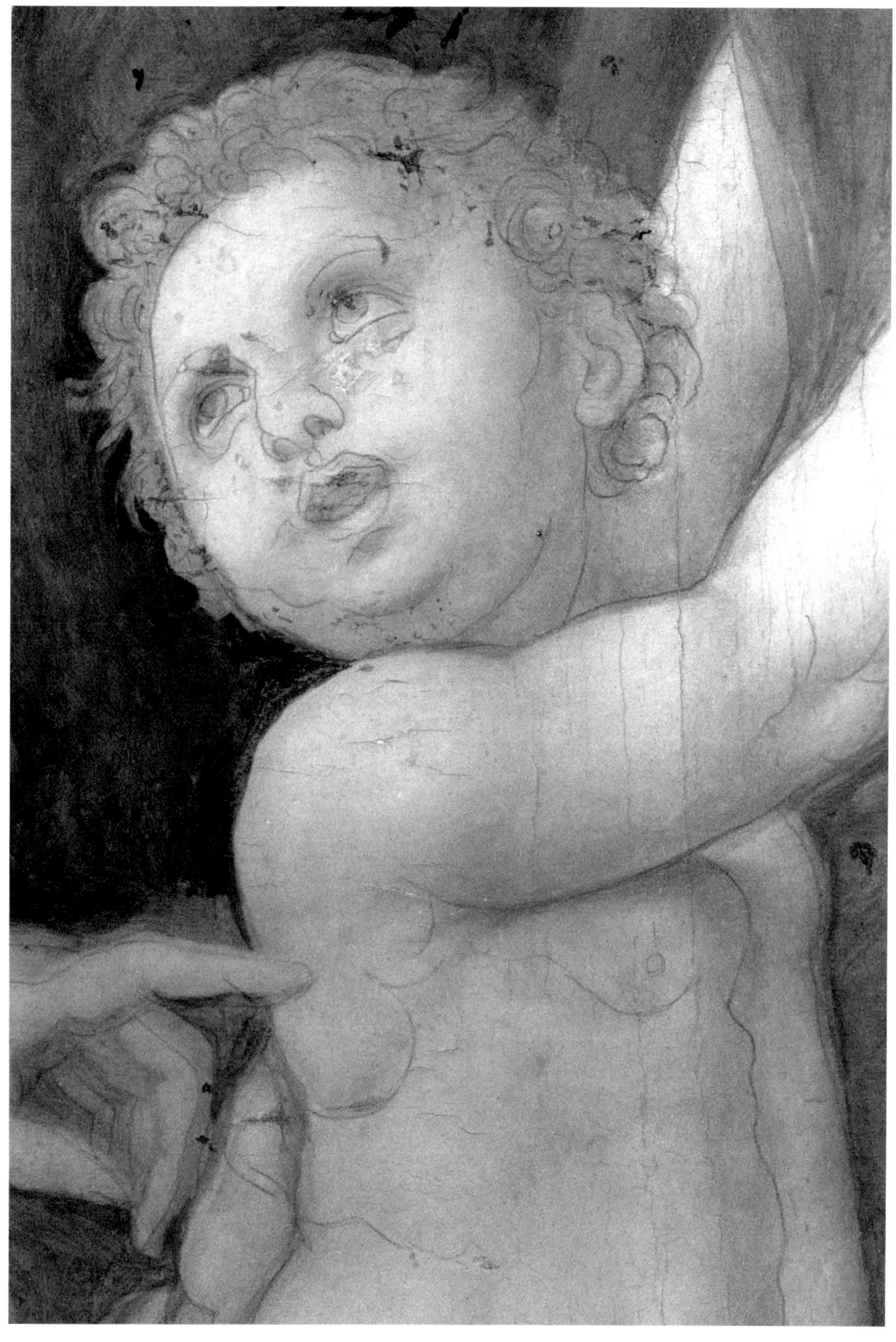

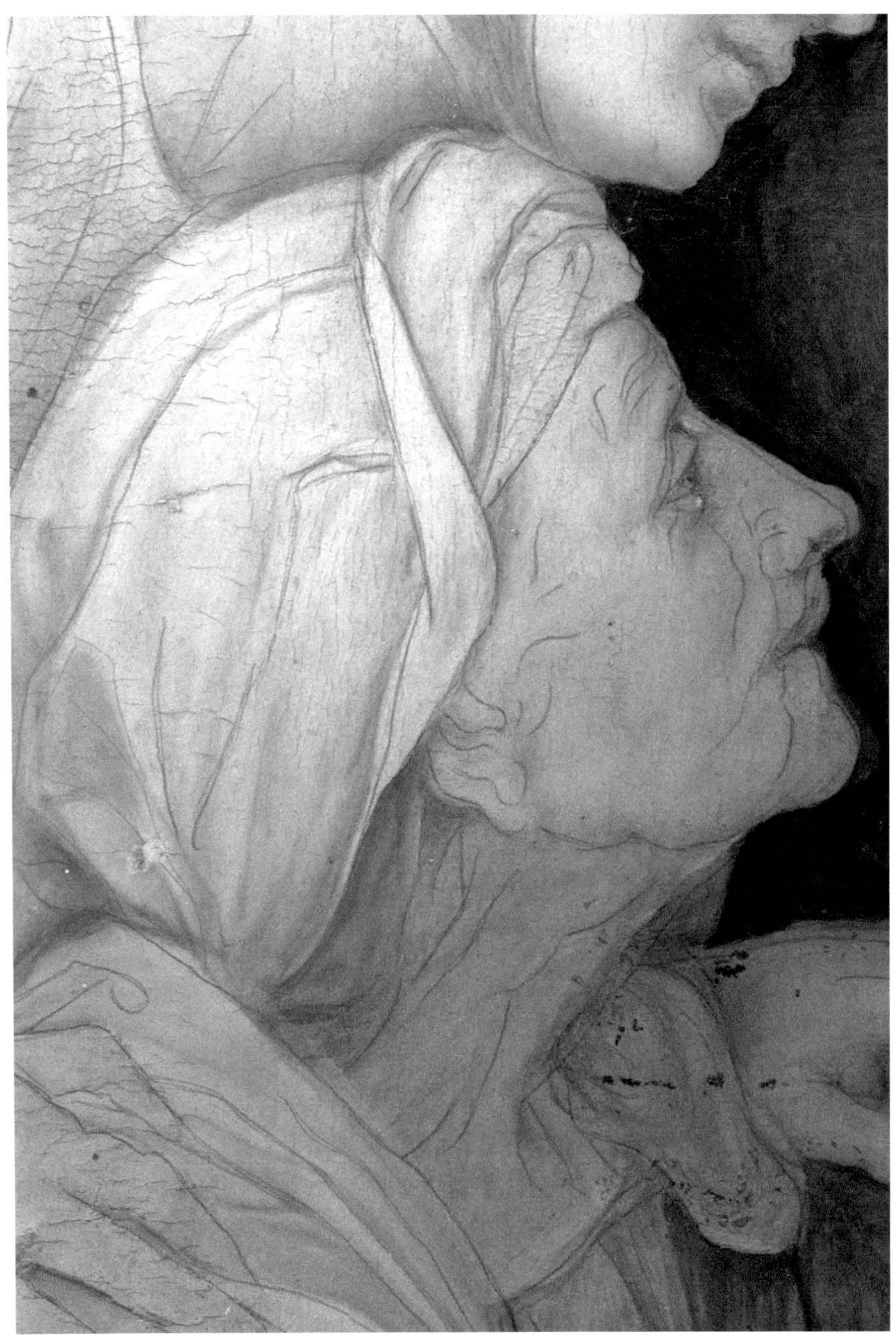

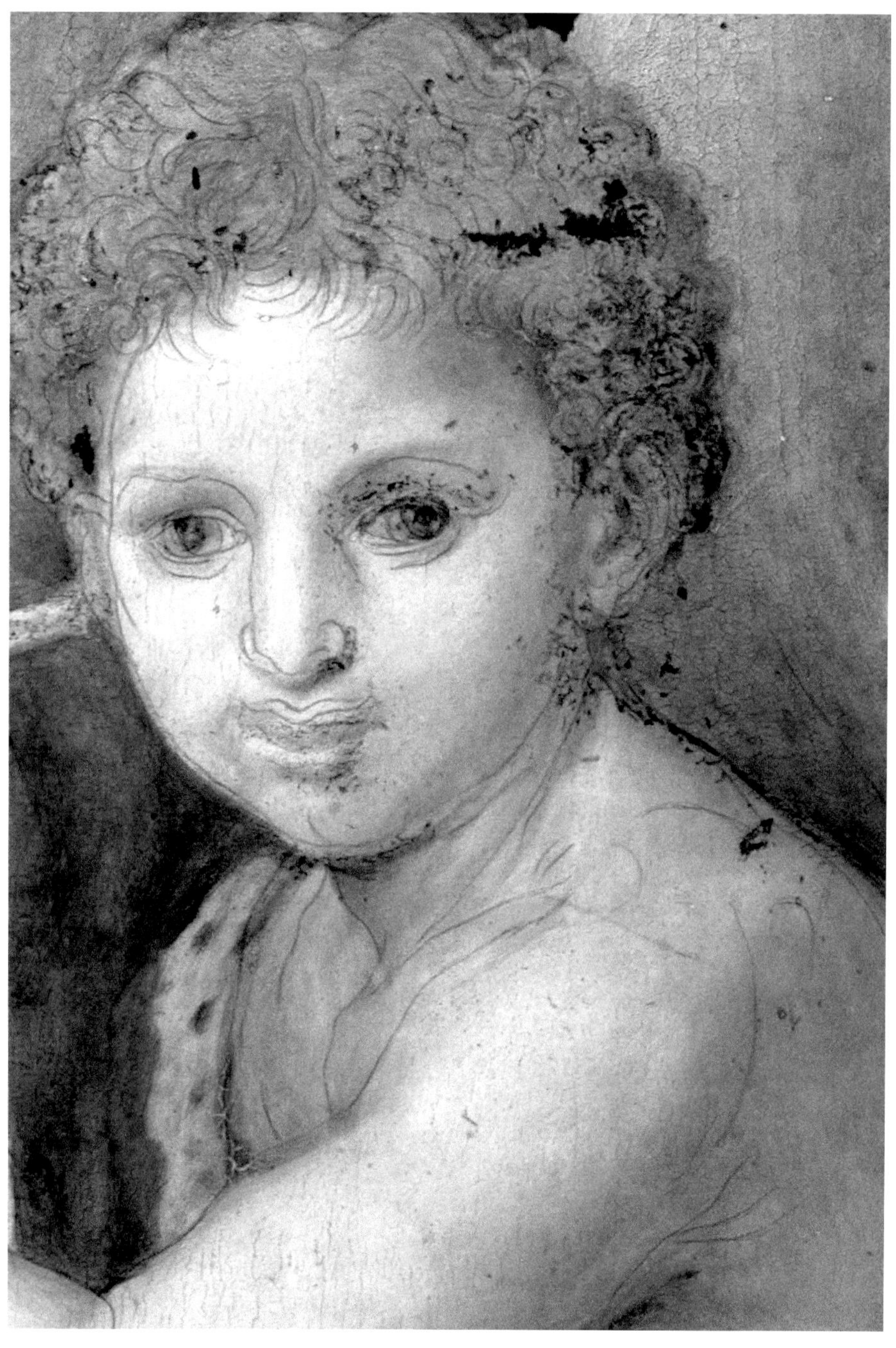

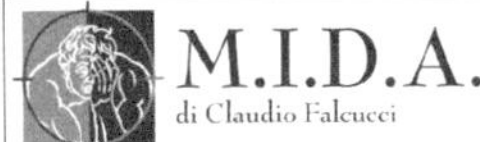

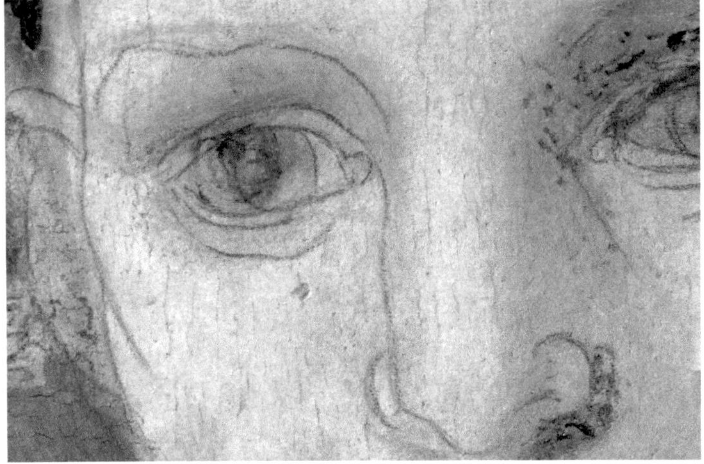

Infrared reflectography - 1800 nm

M.I.D.A. di Claudio Falcucci
Via Leccosa, 15/16 - 00186 Roma - P. IVA 08704231003 - C.F. FLCCLD67E23C858T
Sede legale: via Aprilia, 12 - 00034 Colleferro (Roma)
tel. 06.68803992 - cell. 335.6768683
web site: www.midaonline.com - e-mail: info@midaonline.com

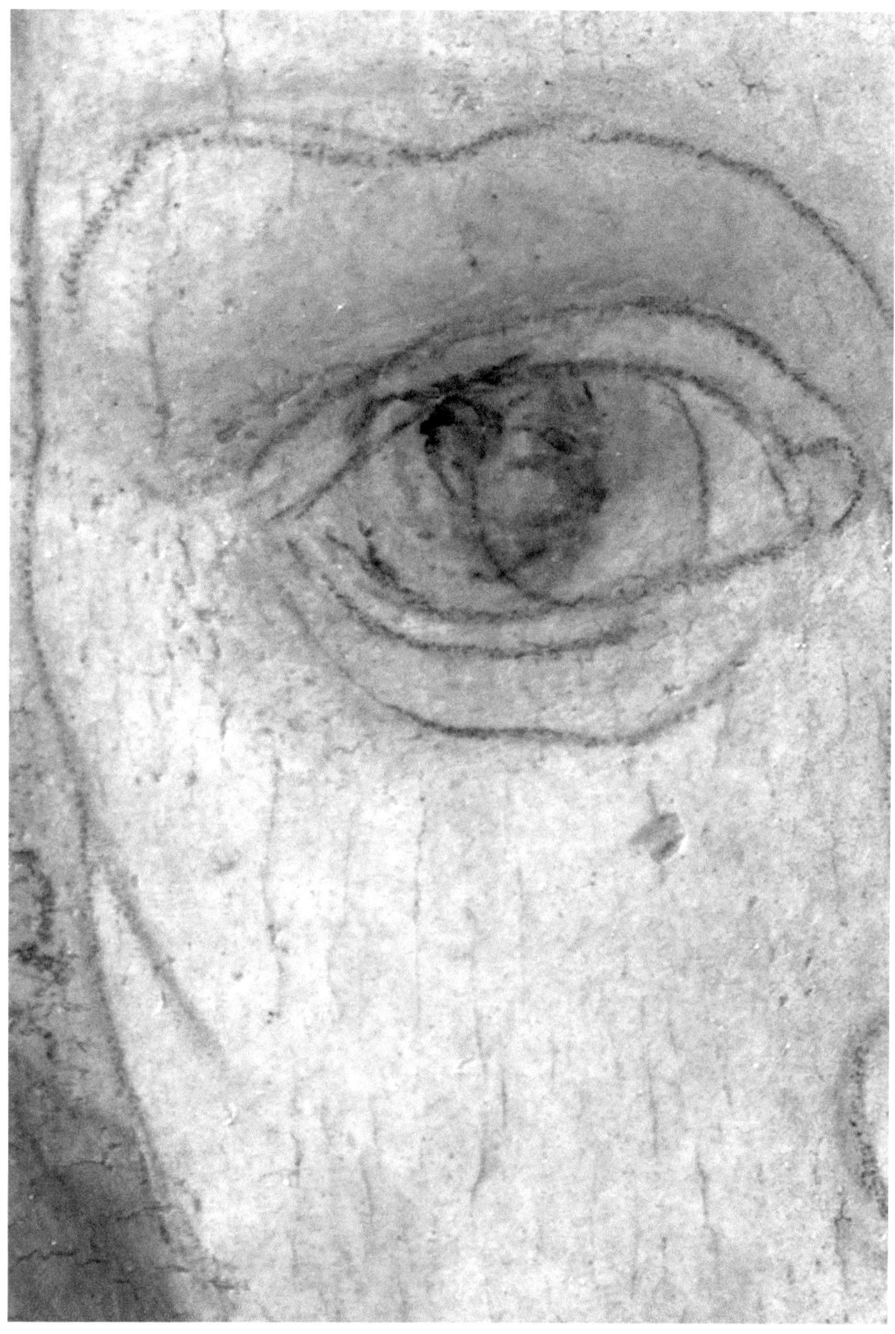

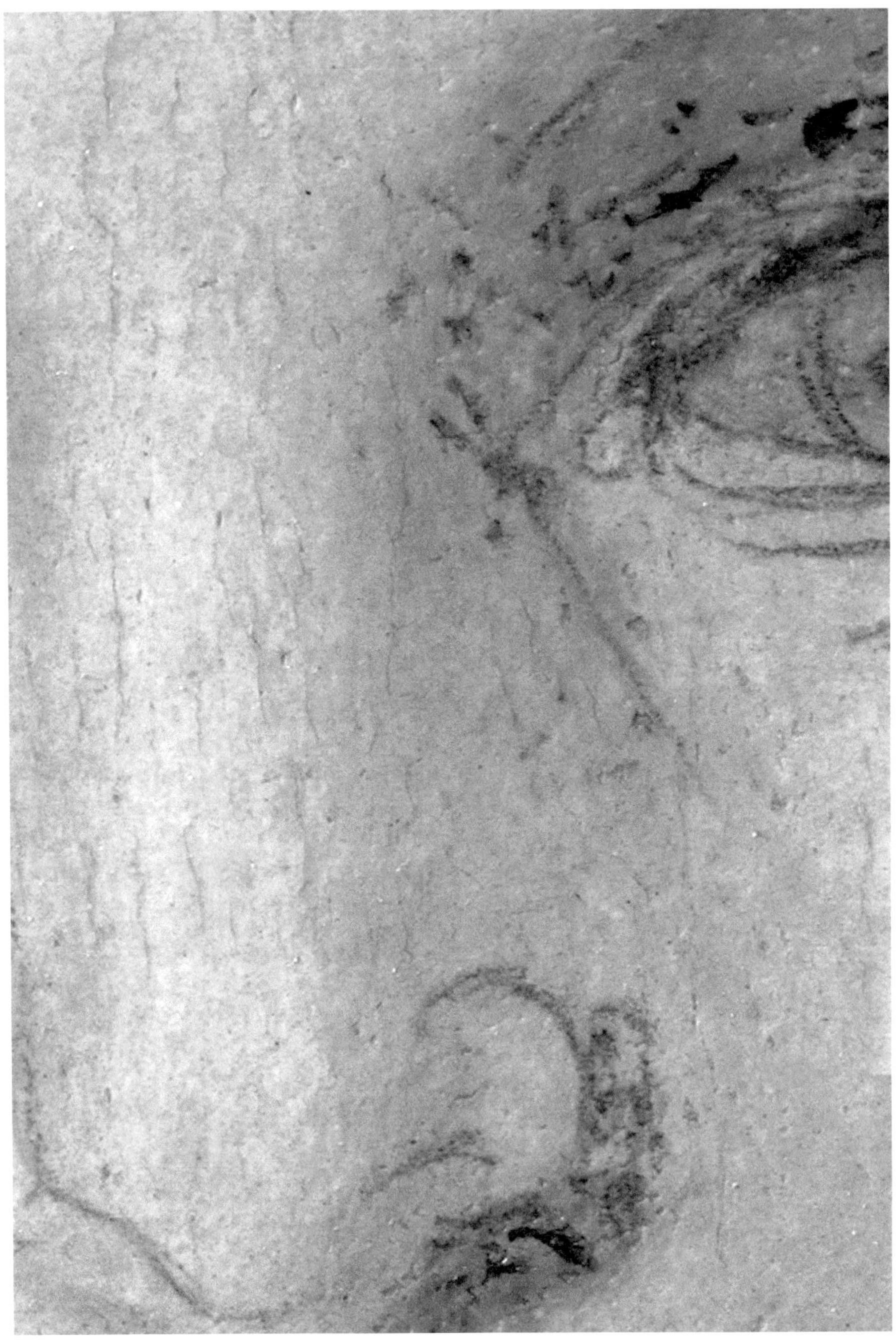

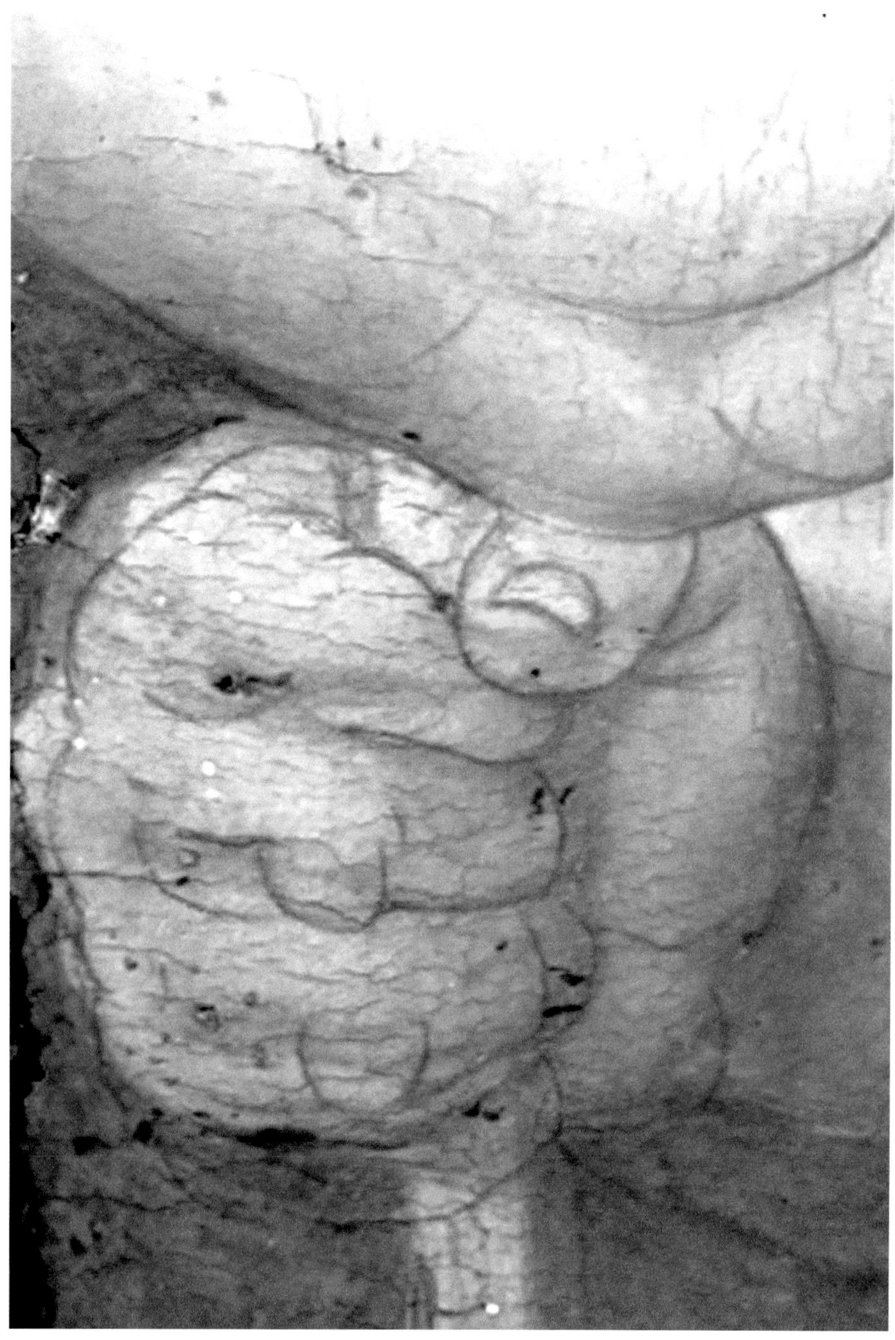

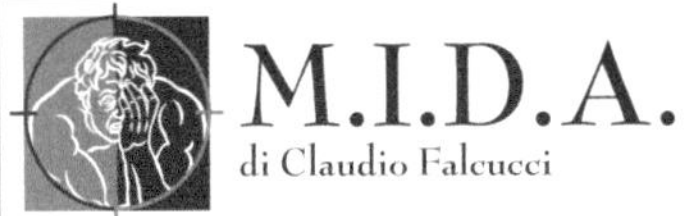

M.I.D.A.
di Claudio Falcucci

Metodologie d'Indagine per la Diagnostica Artistica

Analisi XRF (Fluorescenza dei Raggi X)

Data di analisi:	30 marzo 2010
Punti analizzati:	9
Sorgente primaria:	Tubo radiogeno (anodo W)
Tensione:	40 kV
Corrente:	0.1 mA
Filtro aggiuntivo:	Fe - 70 µm
Tempo di misura:	50 s
Elementi rivelabili:	dal potassio all'uranio

Sono stati analizzati 9 punti selezionati in modo da campionare i colori e le tonalità presenti sull'opera. Precisiamo che l'analisi XRF condotta in aria ed in modo rigorosamente non distruttivo mediante lo spettrometro impiegato, consente di individuare gli elementi chimici di numero atomico superiore a quello del potassio. Sulla base degli elementi rivelati risulta possibile individuare il tipo o i tipi di pigmenti impiegati dall'artista e durante i successivi interventi di restauro per l'ottenimento dei vari colori e delle diverse tonalità. Non possono essere individuati pigmenti contenenti esclusivamente elementi di basso numero atomico, come ad esempio tutti i pigmenti organici ed il blu di lapislazzulo. La presenza di questi pigmenti può però in genere essere dedotta dall'assenza, nel punto analizzato, di altri pigmenti di quel colore. Si precisa inoltre che, essendo un tipo di indagine che si basa sull'individuazione di alcuni elementi chimici, l'analisi XRF non è in grado di distinguere tra di loro pigmenti dello stesso colore e di composizione chimica molto simile, come ad esempio il verderame, la malachite ed il resinato di rame. In tutti questi casi verrà infatti evidenziata solamente la presenza di rame.

I risultati dell'analisi XRF, presentati sotto forma di conteggi e di percentuali relative, non possono essere interpretati in senso quantitativo, ma solamente qualitativo o semiquantitativo, a causa delle disomogeneità caratteristiche di un'opera pittorica e della assoluta non distruttività del tipo di analisi.

Proprio perché i risultati non possono essere interpretati in senso quantitativo, non si è ritenuto opportuno effettuare neppure le correzioni numeriche relative alle efficienze di eccitazione, produzione di fotoni di fluorescenza e di rivelazione per i diversi elementi.

M.I.D.A. di Claudio Falcucci
Via Leccosa, 15-16 - 00186 Roma - P. IVA 08704231003 - C.F. FLCCLD67E23C858T
Sede legale: via Aprilia, 12 - 00034 Colleferro (Roma)
tel. 06.68803992 - cell. 335.6768683
web-site: www.midaonline.com   e-mail: info@midaonline.com

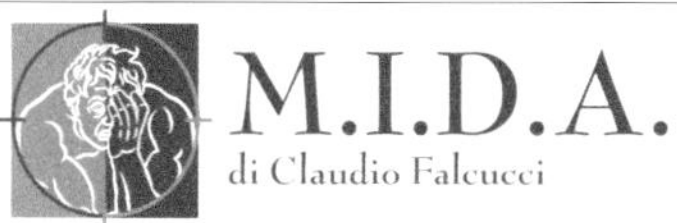

M.I.D.A.
di Claudio Falcucci

Metodologie d'Indagine per la Diagnostica Artistica

Punto: Impa.01

Colore: Giallo

Data di analisi: 30/03/2010

Tempo di misura: 50 secondi

Descrizione: Manica, mezzo tono

	Fe	Sn	Pb
Cont.	97	420	7216
Perc.	1.25	5.43	93.31

Pigmenti individuati: Giallorino, Ocra gialla, Bianco di piombo

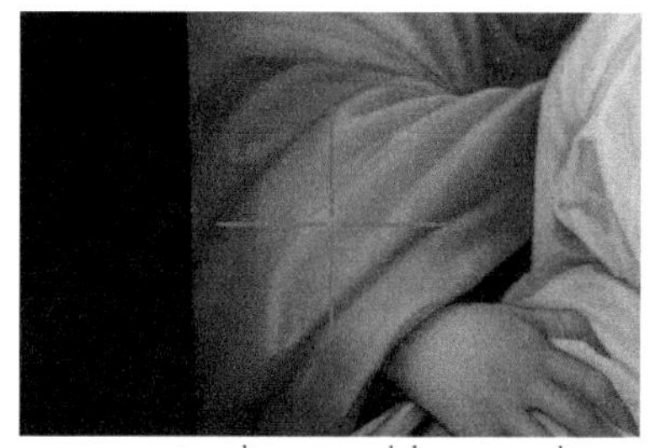

Localizzazione del punto analizzato

Punto: Impa.02

Colore: Azzurro

Data di analisi: 30/03/2010

Tempo di misura: 50 secondi

Descrizione: Velo della Madonna

	Fe	Co	Ni	As	Pb
Cont.	32	125	31	225	6665
Perc.	0.45	1.77	0.44	3.18	94.17

Pigmenti individuati: Blu di smalto, Bianco di piombo, *Oltremare naturale*

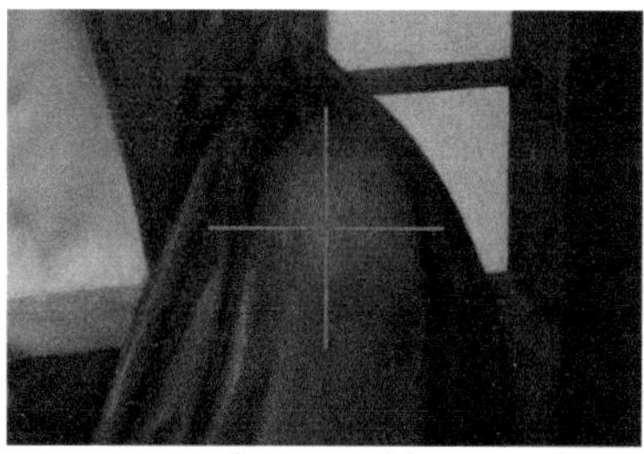

Localizzazione del punto analizzato

M.I.D.A. di Claudio Falcucci
Via Leccosa, 15-16 - 00186 Roma - P. IVA 08704231003 - C.F. FLCCLD67E23C858T
Sede legale: via Aprilia, 12 - 00034 Colleferro (Roma)
tel. 06.68803992 - cell. 335.6768683
web-site: www.midaonline.com e-mail: info@midaonline.com

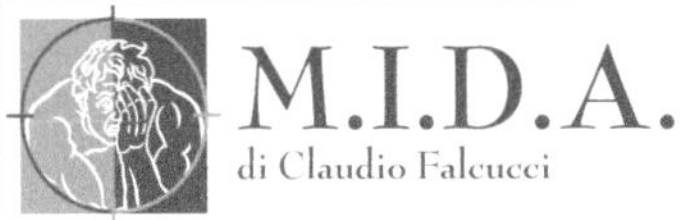

M.I.D.A.
di Claudio Falcucci

Metodologie d'Indagine per la Diagnostica Artistica

Punto: Impa.03

Colore: Azzurro

Data di analisi: 30/03/2010

Tempo di misura: 50 secondi

Descrizione: Velo della Madonna, alterato

	Fe	Co	Ni	As	Pb
Cont.	128	389	145	470	418
Perc.	8.26	25.10	9.35	30.32	26.97

Pigmenti individuati: Blu di smalto, Bianco di piombo, Terre

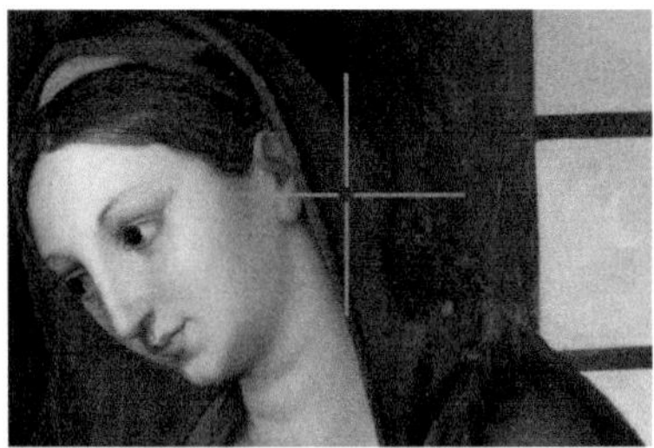

Localizzazione del punto analizzato

Punto: Impa.04

Colore: Incarnato

Data di analisi: 30/03/2010

Tempo di misura: 50 secondi

Descrizione: Guancia del Bambino

	Fe	Hg	Pb
Cont.	21	995	7217
Perc.	0.26	12.09	87.66

Pigmenti individuati: Bianco di piombo, Cinabro, Terre

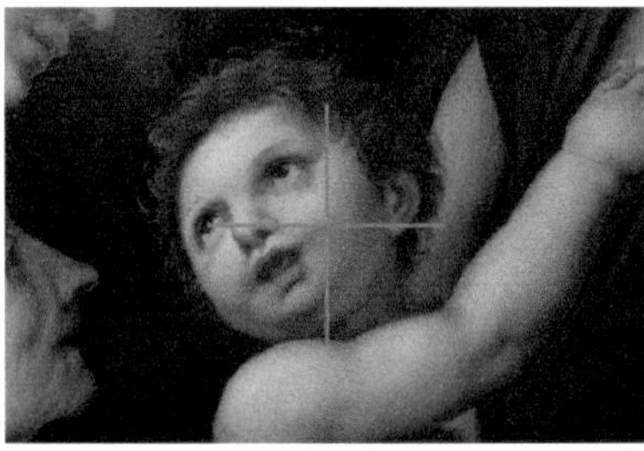

Localizzazione del punto analizzato

M.I.D.A. di Claudio Falcucci
Via Leccosa, 15-16 - 00186 Roma - P. IVA 08704231003 - C.F. FLCCLD07E23C858T
Sede legale: via Aprilia, 12 - 00034 Colleferro (Roma)
tel. 06.68803992 - cell. 335.6768683
website: www.midaonline.com - e-mail: info@midaonline.com

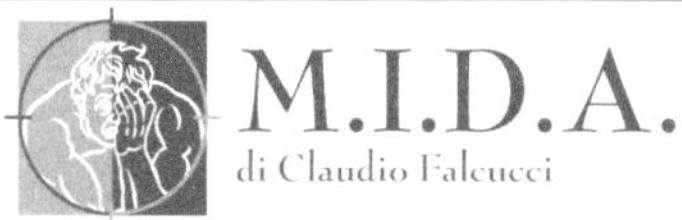

M.I.D.A.
di Claudio Falcucci

Metodologie d'Indagine per la Diagnostica Artistica

Punto: Impa.05

Colore: Rosso

Data di analisi: 30/03/2010

Tempo di misura: 50 secondi

Descrizione: Piega della veste, in ombra

	Ca	Pb
Cont.	41	5852
Perc.	0.70	99.30

Pigmenti individuati: Bianco di piombo, *Lacca rossa*

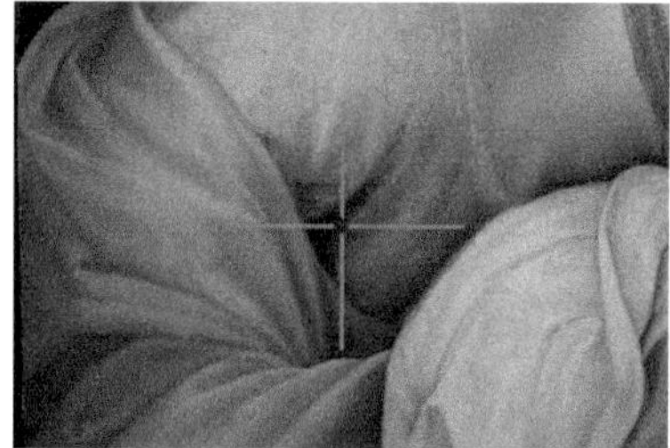

Localizzazione del punto analizzato

Punto: Impa.06

Colore: Rosso

Data di analisi: 30/03/2010

Tempo di misura: 50 secondi

Descrizione: Sedile della Madonna

	Hg	Pb
Cont.	1488	6022
Perc.	19.81	80.19

Pigmenti individuati: Bianco di piombo, Cinabro

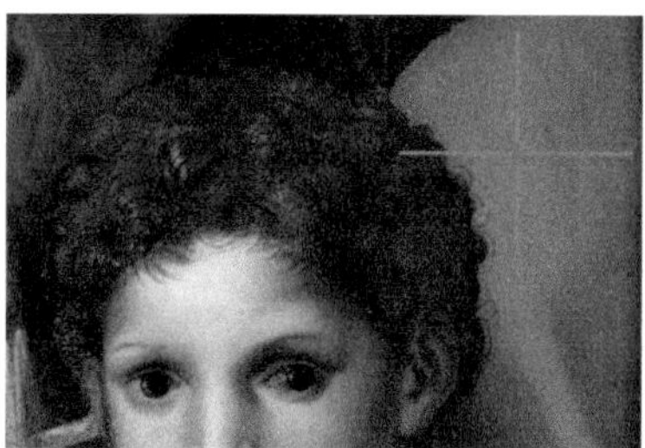

Localizzazione del punto analizzato

M.I.D.A. di Claudio Falcucci
Via Lecosa, 15-16 - 00186 Roma - P.IVA 08704231003 - C.F. FLCCLD67L23C858T
Sede legale: via Aprilia, 12 - 00034 Colleferro (Roma)
tel. 06.68803992 - cell. 335.6768683
web-site: www.midaonline.com - e-mail: info@midaonline.com

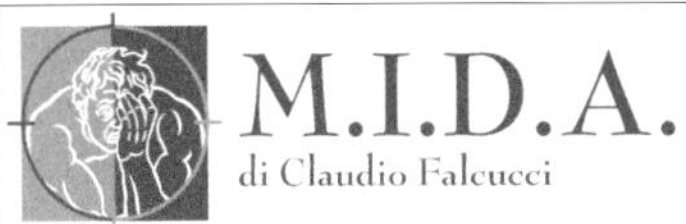

M.I.D.A.
di Claudio Falcucci

Metodologie d'Indagine per la Diagnostica Artistica

Punto: Impa.07

Data di analisi: 30/03/2010

Descrizione: Foglia

Colore: Verde

Tempo di misura: 50 secondi

	Ca	Cu	Pb
Cont.	60	2707	3670
Perc.	0.93	42.05	57.01

Pigmenti individuati: Malachite, Bianco di piombo

Note: Nel punto analizzato potrebbero essere presenti anche pigmenti del tipo dell'acetato di rame e del resinato, non distinguibili dalla malachite sulla base della sola analisi di fluorescenza dei raggi X.

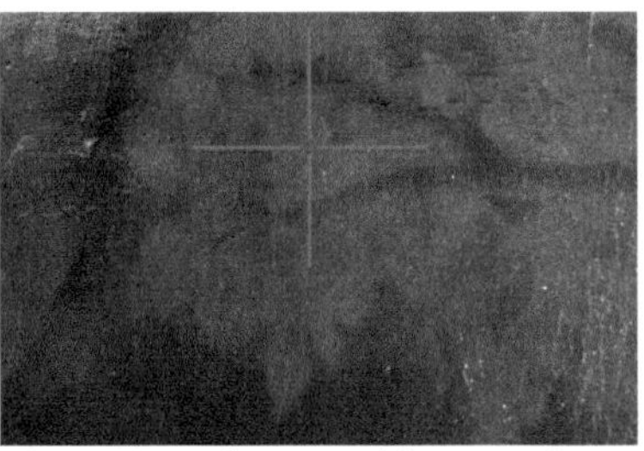

Localizzazione del punto analizzato

Punto: Impa.08

Data di analisi: 30/03/2010

Descrizione: Tenda

Colore: Verde

Tempo di misura: 50 secondi

	Ca	Cu	Hg	Pb
Cont.	61	2414	92	5955
Perc.	0.72	28.33	1.08	69.88

Pigmenti individuati: Malachite, Bianco di piombo

Note: Nel punto analizzato potrebbero essere presenti anche pigmenti del tipo dell'acetato di rame e del resinato, non distinguibili dalla malachite sulla base della sola analisi di fluorescenza dei raggi X.

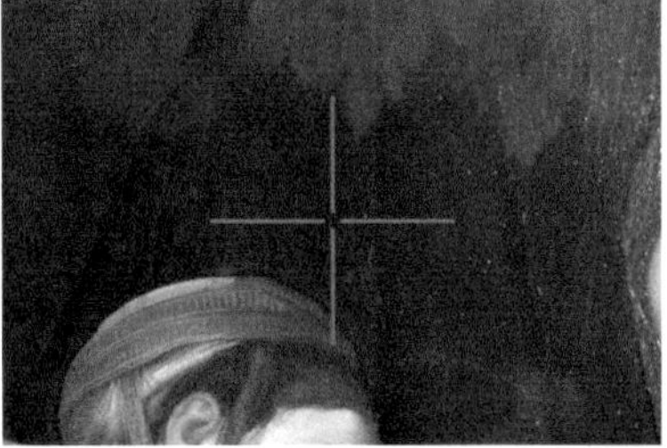

Localizzazione del punto analizzato

M.I.D.A. di Claudio Falcucci
Via Leccosa, 15-16 - 00186 Roma - P. IVA 08704231003 - C.F. FLCCLD67E23C858T
Sede legale: via Aprilia, 12 - 00034 Colleferro (Roma)
tel. 06.68803992 - cell. 335.6768683
web-site: www.midaonline.com - e-mail: info@midaonline.com

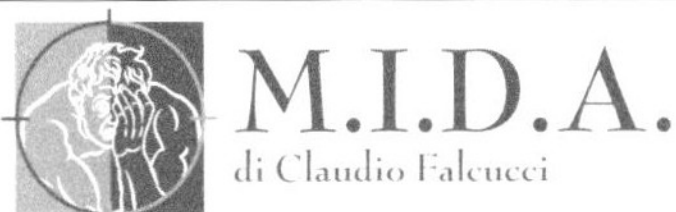

M.I.D.A.
di Claudio Falcucci

Metodologie d'Indagine per la Diagnostica Artistica

Punto: Impa.09

Colore: Azzurro

Data di analisi: 30/03/2010

Tempo di misura: 50 secondi

Descrizione: Manica di sant'Anna, alterato

	Fe	Co	Ni	As	Pb
Cont.	61	176	28	298	4902
Perc.	1.12	3.22	0.51	5.45	89.70

Pigmenti individuati: Blu di smalto, Bianco di piombo

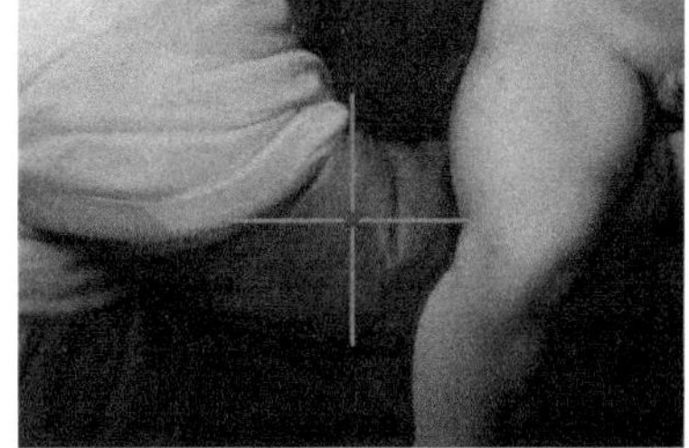

Localizzazione del punto analizzato

M.I.D.A. di Claudio Falcucci
Via Leccosa, 15-16 - 00186 Roma - P. IVA 08704231003 - C.F. FLCCLD67L23C858I
Sede legale: via Aprilia, 12 - 00034 Colleferro (Roma)
tel. 06.68803992 - cell. 335.6708083
web-site: www.midaonline.com - e-mail: info@midaonline.com

Raffael und seine Zeit / Raphael And His Time

Herausgegeben von / Edited by Jürg Meyer zur Capellen

Band / Vol. 1   Jürg Meyer zur Capellen / Claudio Falcucci: The *Portrait of Baldassare Castiglione &*
Madonna dell'Impannata Northwick. Two Studies on Raphael. 2011.

www.peterlang.de

Autor/Author

Druckreif / Ready for press	☐
Nach Korrektur druckreif / **O.K. with corrections**	☐
Unterschrift / **Signature:**	
Datum / Date:	